Seabird Colony Survey Report 2011

Kenai Fjords National Park and Alaska Maritime National Wildlife Refuge

Natural Resource Report NPS/KEFJ/NRDS—2012/312

Monika Parsons

National Park Service
P.O. Box 1727
Seward, AK 99664

Laura Phillips, Jennifer Curl, Leslie Adams

National Park Service
P.O. Box 1727
Seward, AK 99664

April 2012

U.S. Department of the Interior
National Park Service
Natural Resource Stewardship and Science
Fort Collins, Colorado

The National Park Service, Natural Resource Stewardship and Science office in Fort Collins, Colorado publishes a range of reports that address natural resource topics of interest and applicability to a broad audience in the National Park Service and others in natural resource management, including scientists, conservation and environmental constituencies, and the public.

The Natural Resource Data Series is intended for the timely release of basic data sets and data summaries. Care has been taken to assure accuracy of raw data values, but a thorough analysis and interpretation of the data has not been completed. Consequently, the initial analyses of data in this report are provisional and subject to change.

All manuscripts in the series receive the appropriate level of peer review to ensure that the information is scientifically credible, technically accurate, appropriately written for the intended audience, and designed and published in a professional manner.

Data in this report were collected and analyzed using methods based on established, peer-reviewed protocols and were analyzed and interpreted within the guidelines of the protocols.

Views, statements, findings, conclusions, recommendations, and data in this report do not necessarily reflect views and policies of the National Park Service, U.S. Department of the Interior. Mention of trade names or commercial products does not constitute endorsement or recommendation for use by the U.S. Government.

This report is available from Kenai Fjords National Park, Resource Management Division and the Natural Resource Publications Management website (http://www.nature.nps.gov/publications/nrpm/).

Please cite this publication as:

Parsons, M., L. Phillips, J. Curl and L. Adams. 2012. Seabird colony survey report 2011: Kenai Fjords National Park and Alaska Maritime National Wildlife Refuge. Natural Resource Data Series NPS/KEFJ/NRDS—2012/312. National Park Service, Fort Collins, Colorado.

NPS 186/113584, April 2012

Contents

Figures

Tables

Abstract

Seabird colony surveys have not been regularly conducted in Kenai Fjords National Park (KEFJ) since its inception in 1980. A 2006 Interagency General Agreement led to cooperative seabird colony surveys along the eastern coast of the Kenai Peninsula in KEFJ and the Alaska Maritime National Wildlife Refuge (AMNWR) in 2007, the first time since 1986 that seabird colonies had been surveyed in KEFJ. Since 2007 KEFJ staff has continued annual surveys of seabird colonies in KEFJ and AMNWR at some level. In 2011 we began intensively monitoring select colonies as part of a cooperative interagency project with AMNWR and University of Alaska Fairbanks to identify spatial and temporal variability of colonial seabirds within this region. We conducted shoreline surveys of the KEFJ coast to identify new seabird colonies, performed whole colony counts of most historic colonies, conducted repeated counts of historic black-legged kittiwake photo plots, and established new survey plots for cormorant species (red-faced, pelagic and double-crested), black-legged kittiwakes, common murres and glaucous-winged gulls. Coastline surveys were conducted between 15 June and 29 July by two observers from a 14' inflatable zodiac, from a 19' rigid hulled inflatable "Auklet" or from the flying bridge of the 53' M/V Serac travelling at 5-10 knots within 100 meters of shore. We considered two birds present standing onshore within 100 meters of each other a colony for puffin and murre species, two nests with attending birds within 100 meters of each other a colony for all other species. Whole colony counts were conducted by two observers from the M/V Serac or Auklet. For puffins, murres, and gulls individual birds present on a colony were counted. For kittiwakes and cormorants, we counted both nests and individual birds. We defined nests as an adult or chick sitting or standing over nesting material. Observers broke colonies larger than 300 birds into segments to ease counting. Counts were repeated until both observers obtained counts within 10%. Results from the current survey were compiled with data from previous surveys in 2010 (Phillips and McFarland 2010), 2009 (McFarland et al. 2009), 2008 (Hahr 2009), 2007 (Hahr 2008), 1986 (Nishimoto and Rice 1987) and 1976 (Bailey 1977) to examine apparent changes in colony size and composition. All KEFJ colonies were counted at least once. Eight historic and two newly established black-legged kittiwake plots in the Chiswell Islands, nine newly established common murre plots, seven newly established cormorant plots and twelve newly established glaucous-winged gull plots were counted on multiple days using the same procedure used for whole colony counts. We discovered 18 new seabird colonies (eight puffin species, four cormorant species, three mew gull and three glaucous-winged gull colonies) and failed to detect breeding activity at seven of 35 historic colonies surveyed. Direct comparisons with historic survey data is limited because of varying survey methods; however, descriptive comparisons of limited count data reflect the apparent variability in colony attendance since 1976 with an apparent increase in glaucous-winged gulls throughout the survey area. The number of kittiwakes nesting within eight historic plots in the Chiswell Islands has decreased since 2008 but is still greater than the total number breeding within the same plots in 1992. An intensive survey effort including repeated counts of plots will be employed again 2012.

Acknowledgments

We would like to thank Captain Jamie Thompton and deckhand Marybeth Phillis on the M/V Serac. We also appreciate Christine Hunter and Kristen Steinmetzer's help with seabird counts. The logistical support of Mark Kansteiner and Jason Flowers was invaluable in helping our field season run smoothly. We also appreciate Fritz Klasner and Leslie Slater's project support and Heather Coletti for her editorial skills.

Introduction

Almost all seabirds are colonial nesters (Wittenberger and Hunt 1985), which allows for relatively easy survey efforts during the breeding season. These surveys can aid region-wide ecosystem analyses as seabirds are useful indicators of long and short term marine conditions, including regime shifts and changes due to climate change (Piatt et al. 2007). Seabird colonies on the southern Kenai Peninsula have not been surveyed frequently or consistently; however, a 2006 General Agreement between the National Park Service (NPS), U.S. Fish and Wildlife Service (USFWS) and the National Oceanic and Atmospheric Administration (NOAA) sought to increase cooperation and efficiency between agencies where they share nearby coastal waters (USDI 2006). This agreement prompted a 2007 interagency survey of 14 seabird colonies along the southwest coast of the Kenai Peninsula by NPS, Kenai Fjords National Park (KEFJ) and USFWS, Alaska Maritime National Wildlife Refuge (AMNWR) staff (Hahr 2008). A second cooperative survey effort occurred in 2008 when two KEFJ colonies (Bear Glacier Point and Aialik Cape) were surveyed and black-legged kittiwake and common murres were counted in the Chiswell Islands (Hahr 2009). In 2009 staff from both agencies conducted surveys of breeding seabirds at colonies on the mainland within KEFJ (n=17) and on islands within the AMNWR (n=18) (McFarland et al. 2009). In 2010 KEFJ staff surveyed four colony locations in KEFJ and seven colony locations in AMNWR (Phillips and McFarland 2010). In contrast to USFWS protocols (USFWS 1998, 2000a, 2000b, 2000c) that AMNWR uses to determine population trends, logistical constraints limited our 2009 and 2010 surveys to single visits to determine presence of nesting seabirds at historic colony sites. We used the results from the 2009 and 2010 surveys to estimate relative abundance in conjunction with historical data (McFarland et al. 2009, Phillips and McFarland 2010).

Previous to the 2006 Agreement, the coastline of the southern Kenai Peninsula was surveyed by Bailey (1977) prior to the designation of KEFJ and AMNWR by Alaska National Interest Lands Conservation Act (ANILCA 1980); and a re-survey of this area, encompassing 610 miles, was performed in 1986 (Nishimoto and Rice 1987). The 1986 survey focused on total species counts within 11 coastal units, lumping nesting birds with roosting birds and those on the water unless large aggregations of nesting birds were noted. Surveys were also conducted in the Pye Islands (AMNWR) in 1990 and Chiswell Islands in the early 1990's to identify potential impacts to seabirds from the Exxon Valdez Oil Spill (Nysewander et al. 1993, Dragoo 1994).

In 2011, KEFJ staff in cooperation with AMNWR and University of Alaska Fairbanks began a three year intensive seabird study to establish monitoring protocols for breeding seabirds in KEFJ and adjacent areas of AMNWR. The goals of this study are to:

- Document previously undetected seabird colonies by systematically surveying the coastline within KEFJ.

- Determine the status (occupied or unoccupied) and species composition of all seabird colonies documented in surveys from 1976-2010.

- Produce GIS maps of the locations of seabird colonies in KEFJ and adjacent AMNWR islands.

- Develop statistically valid protocols for monitoring long term presence and abundance of colony nesting seabirds within KEFJ and adjacent AMNWR islands.

This report presents a summary of data gathered in 2011 with preliminary comparisons to seabird surveys from previous years.

Methods

Site Selection

The south coast of the Kenai Peninsula is characterized by steep fjords composed of greywacke, slate or granite. The Harding Icefield and associated glaciers cover approximately 1,900 km^2 of the Kenai Peninsula (Giffen et al. 2009). The climate along the coast is maritime, with mild temperatures and high rainfall due to orographic uplift and driven by the Aleutian Low (Lindsay and Klasner 2009). Numerous steep islands and island groups are located close to the mainland.

Kenai Fjords National Park (KEFJ) (Figure 1) was established in 1980 to protect the Harding Icefield, its associated fjords and the marine mammals and birds that depend on them (ANILCA 1980). KEFJ administers approximately 2,450 km^2; its boundaries include an additional 225 km^2 managed primarily by the State of Alaska and Port Graham Native Corporation.

The Alaska Maritime National Wildlife Refuge (AMNWR) (Figure 1) encompasses almost 20,000 km^2 and 2,500 islands, stretching along most of the coastline of Alaska. The AMNWR was established primarily to conserve the animals and habitats found within its boundaries, and to provide for subsistence use, conduct research on marine resources and ensure water quality within the refuge (ANILCA 1980).

All of the seabird colonies we surveyed in 2011 were within KEFJ or AMNWR. The study area stretched from Yalik Point in Nuka Bay (59.918°N, 150.586°W) to Bear Glacier Point in Resurrection Bay (59.893°N, 149.553°W) and encompassed nearby islands including the Chiswell Island group, one of the Pye Islands, and numerous other islands under the jurisdiction of AMNWR (Figure 2). All lands within the KEFJ boundary including inholdings were included in the survey area. The Chiswell Islands have some of the largest and most diverse breeding seabird colonies in the Kenai Fjords region (Bailey 1977). The U.S. Fish and Wildlife Service established black-legged kittiwake photo plots on Beehive, Beehive B, Chiswell and Matushka Island in 1992. We established additional population monitoring plots for black-legged kittiwakes, common murres, glaucous-winged gulls, and red-faced, double-crested and pelagic cormorants along the western side of Resurrection Bay, Aialik Cape, the Chiswell Islands and the outer coast.

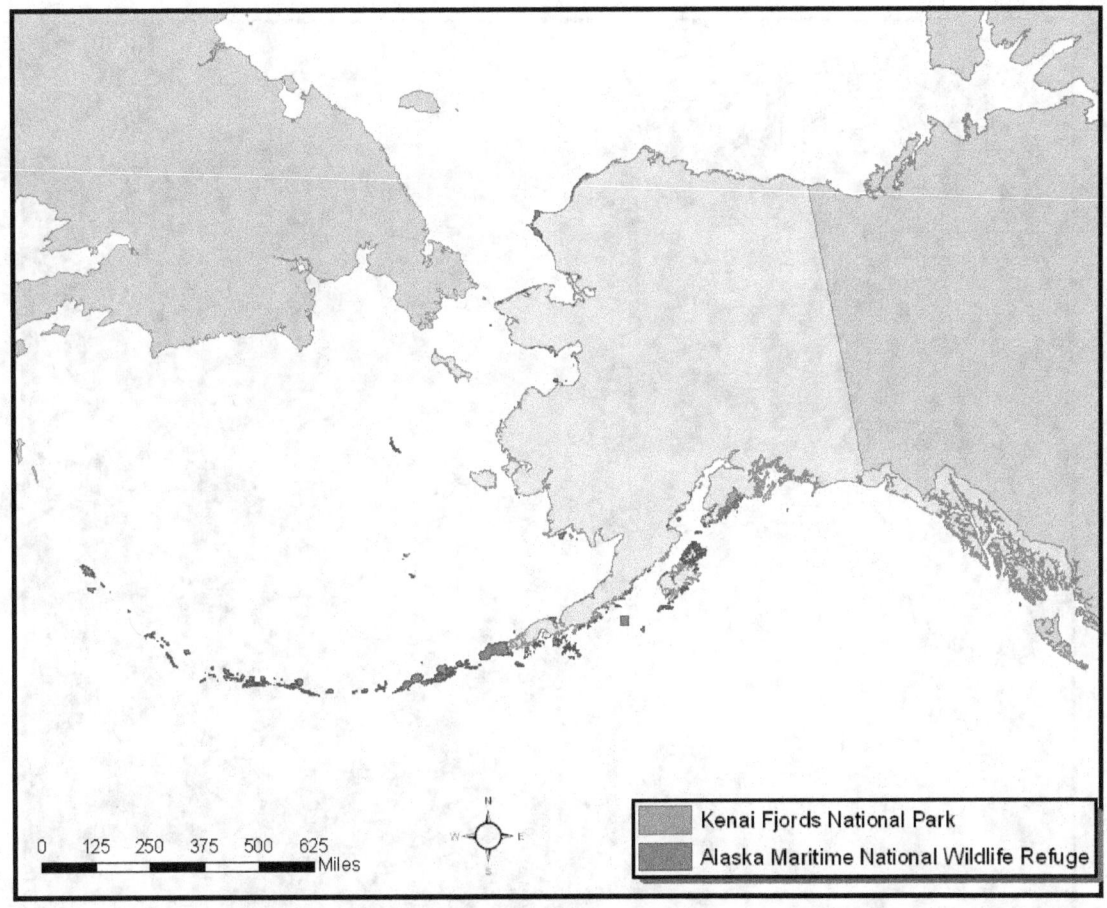

Figure 1. Location of Kenai Fjords National Park and the Alaska Maritime National Wildlife Refuge in Alaska.

Coastline Surveys

We conducted coastline surveys from Yalik Point to Bear Glacier Point to inventory the current location and distribution of colonies within KEFJ. We surveyed the mainland shoreline for seabird colonies from the flying bridge of the 53' M/V Serac, from the 19' ridged hulled inflatable "Auklet", or from a 14' inflatable zodiac. Nearshore islands were surveyed opportunistically, usually in locations where historic colonies were documented. Surveys were performed between the hours of 0800 and 1900 from 15 June to 29 July in conditions varying from 0-6' swell and sunny to hard rain.

We drove the vessels along the coastline within 100 meters of shore at 5-10 knots. Two observers scanned the coastline using 10x40 image stabilized binoculars and 10x42 binoculars. A colony was defined as two or more individuals (puffins and murres) or nests with an attending adult (kittiwakes, gulls and cormorants) within 100 meters of each other. We recorded locations of new colonies with a GPS unit, counted the number of individuals present, estimated vegetation cover, vegetation type, cliff height, aspect, and substrate. We recorded our GPS locations using NAD 1983 datum.

3

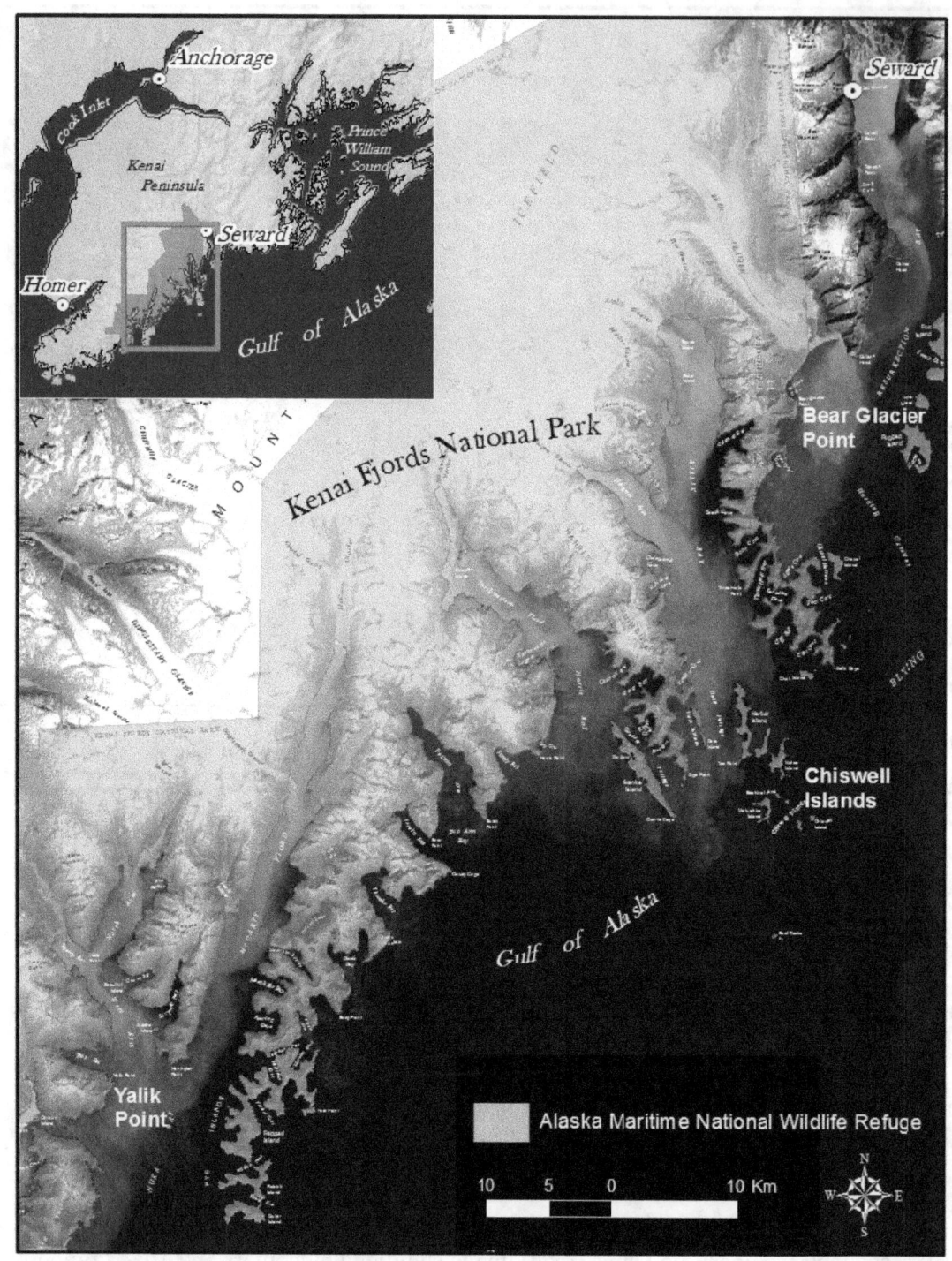

Figure 2. Map of the study area in Kenai Fjords National Park and Alaska Maritime National Wildlife Refuge with place names.

Whole Colony Counts

We conducted whole colony counts of known colonies identified from the USFWS Seabird Colony Database, surveys conducted in the Kenai Fjords area between 1976 and 2010, and colonies identified during shoreline surveys (Figure 3, Figure 4). To determine the number of breeding birds attending a colony we conducted counts from the flying bridge of the 53' M/V Serac, from the19' ridged hulled inflatable "Auklet", or from a 14' inflatable zodiac. Counts were conducted between the hours of 0800 and 1900 in swell ranging from 0-8' and weather conditions ranging from sun to light rain between 13 June and 5 August.

For each survey, we considered all adults of every species present within the colony area to be attending the colony. Adults standing in the intertidal zone and chicks were not included in counts of individuals. Observers counted individual birds at colonies using 10x40 image stabilized binoculars. For black-legged kittiwakes and all cormorant species, we also counted nests with an attending adult or chick. When a break of more than 100 meters occurred between neighboring birds, we designated a new colony location and counted the adjacent colony separately.

We conducted replicate counts of adults and nests at colonies on separate days, generally following the protocols outlined in the USFWS protocols for population inventories of ledge-nesting seabirds (USFWS 2000a). For abundant species (glaucous-winged gulls, cormorant spp., and common murres) two observers independently counted individuals attending a colony during each visit and repeated counts until they obtained counts within 10% of each other. A single observer completed one count for burrow and crevice nesting species (horned and tufted puffins) which were present on the cliffs in low numbers with the majority of individuals hidden from view in burrows. The USFWS protocols (USFWS 2000a) recommends 5-10 replicates per colony, preferably on different days, between the hours of 1100 and 1800 to determine population trends. It also recommends two observer counts to be within 5% of each other. Due to logistical constraints, our protocols differed from that of the USFWS in that our replicate counts varied from the recommended 5-10 and our two observers counted to within 10%, not 5% of each other. Given this, the results presented in this report should be considered valid for relative abundance measurements but not detection of long-term trends.

Results from the current survey were compiled with data from previous surveys in 2010 (Phillips and McFarland 2010), 2009 (McFarland et al. 2009), 2008 (Hahr 2009), 2007 (Hahr 2008), 1986 (Nishimoto and Rice 1987) and 1976 (Bailey 1977) to describe apparent changes in colony size and composition. The data for 2007-2010 are single counts of each colony. The 1986 surveys lumped sections of coastline together as single counts and in 1976 surveys included counts of birds on the water near the shore as well as burrow surveys for puffins. We only used counts of observed nests and adults on land for comparisons among years, omitting the estimated total associated birds for each colony found in the original reports.

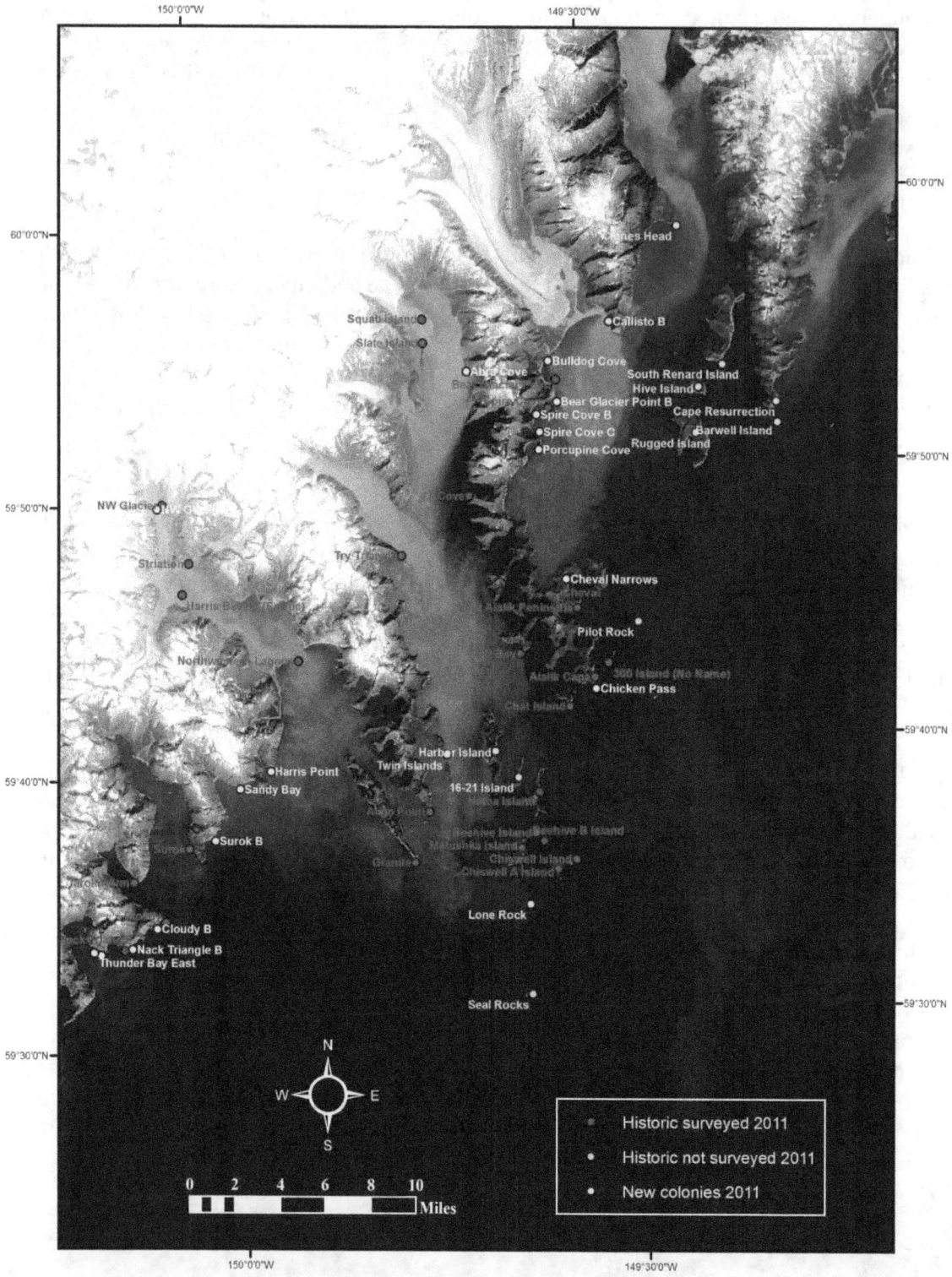

Figure 3. Seabird colonies in or adjacent to the northern half of the Kenai Fjords National Park coastline. Red dots represent known colonies in the area that were resurveyed in 2011, blue dots represent known colonies that were not surveyed in 2011, and yellow dots represent new colonies discovered in 2011.

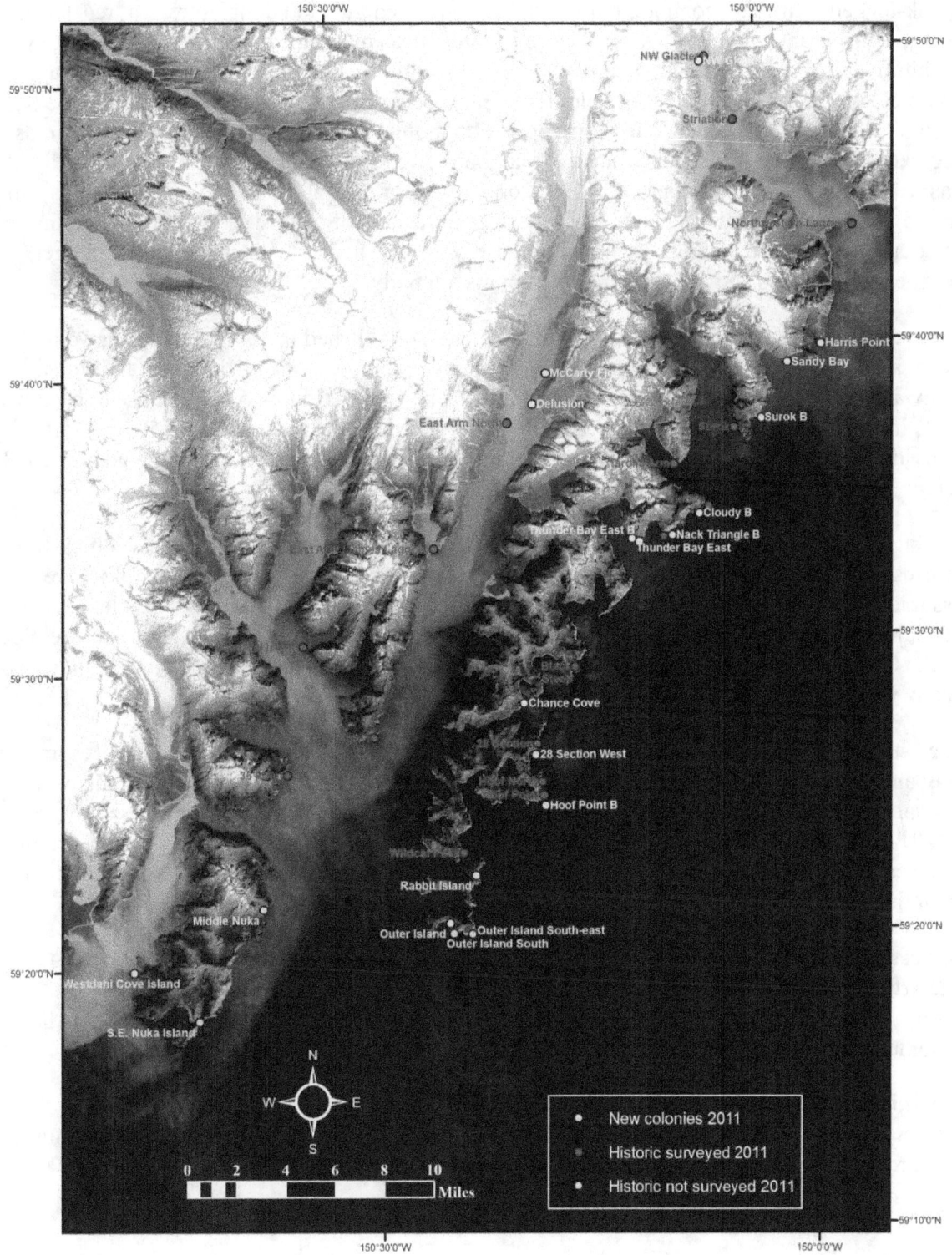

Figure 4. Seabird colonies in or adjacent to the southern half of the Kenai Fjords National Park coastline.

Plot Establishment and Counts

Black-legged kittiwake, common murre, glaucous-winged gull and double-crested, red-faced and pelagic cormorant colonies were very large in some areas making counting the entire colony prohibitively time consuming. Due to logistical constraints associated with visiting remote colonies, we designated subsets of colonies as plots according to protocols outlined by the USFWS (2000a) to facilitate long term population monitoring. A sample plot was defined as "a segment of cliff nesting habitat which; 1) may be viewed from the same location repeatedly, 2) has readily identifiable boundaries, and 3) contains fewer than 300 birds" (USFWS 2000a). In future years, counts of these plots will be used as indicators of colony growth or decline instead of counting the entire colony. Establishing these plots will make it possible to survey larger numbers of colonies and conduct multiple counts annually.

Observers counted eight black-legged kittiwake plots established in 1992 on the Chiswell Islands, using the same protocol as for whole colony counts. We established two additional kittiwake plots on Matushka Island and Unnamed Chiswell A (Figure 5). We chose to establish plots in areas easily identified by physical features and that contained between 50 and 150 individuals. We compared our counts of the eight historic plots with counts completed in 2008 (Hahr 2009) and in 1992 (Dragoo 1994).

During ten days of surveying in the Chiswell Islands in 2011, we only detected two thick-billed murres roosting on Beehive B Island and did not detect any incubating eggs. Therefore we assumed that common murres were the predominant murre species in the Chiswell Islands and considered all murres counted to be common murres. We established nine common murre plots in the Chiswell Islands (Figure 6) at sites with ledges attended by adult murres and bounded by easily identified physical features.

We established eight cormorant plots in the Chiswell Islands, Aialik Cape, Western Resurrection Bay and the Outer Coast (Figure 7). Pelagic cormorants and double-crested cormorants were the primary species present in cormorant plots. Red-faced cormorants were largely absent from plots in 2011because they either failed to breed or bred in locations outside the study area. Cormorant plots covered larger areas than kittiwake and murre plots and in some cases were synonymous with the whole colony at a location.

We established twelve glaucous-winged gull plots from Resurrection Bay (Cheval Island) to McArthur Pass (Steep Point) (Figure 8). Plots were chosen to contain at least 50 birds and no more than 300. On small colonies the plot encompassed the entire area of the colony. On larger colonies and colonies that were spread out, we established multiple plots.

Permits and Archiving

All related project materials are permanently housed in the Kenai Fjords National Park museum and archive collection under accession number KEFJ-00269.

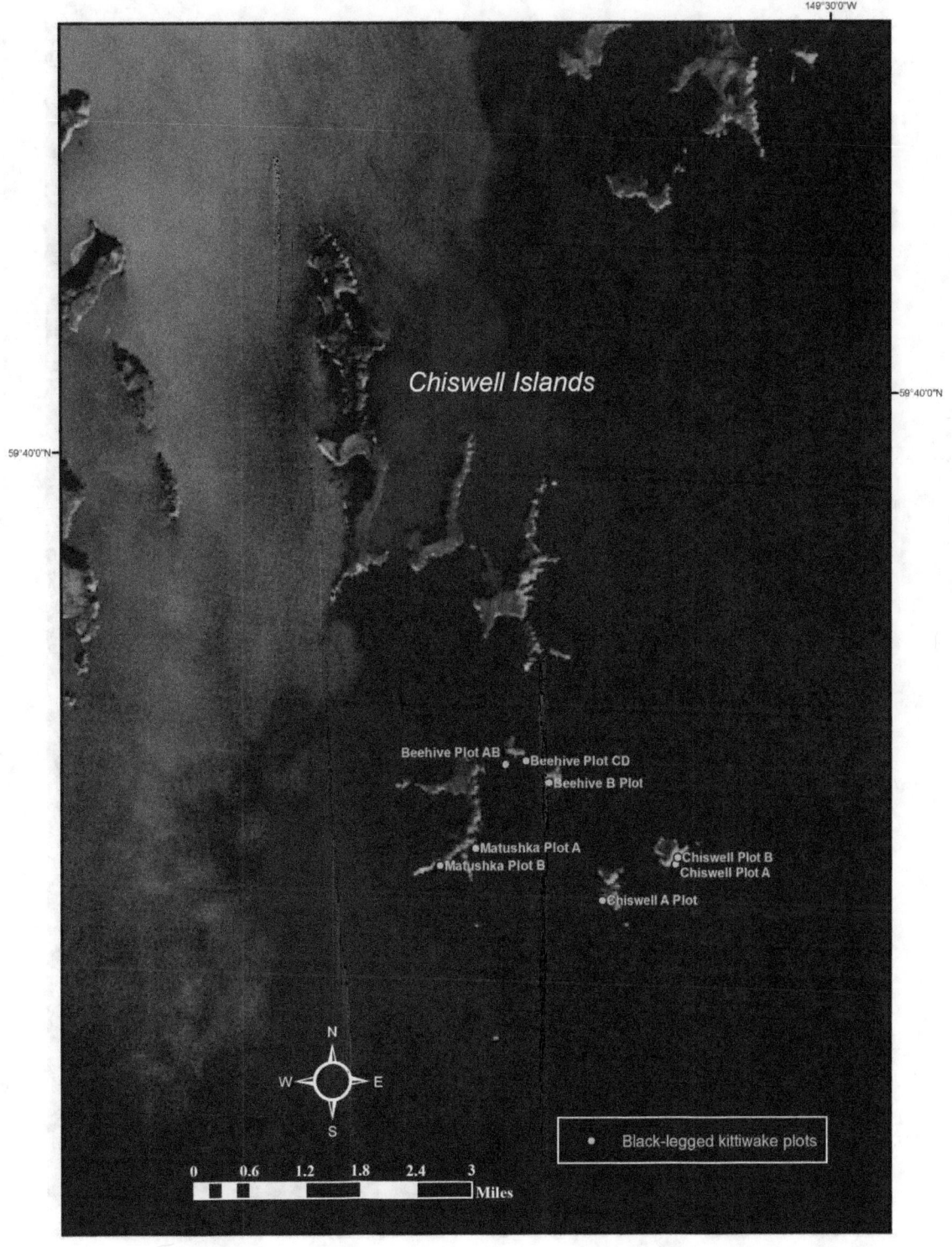

Figure 5. Location of black-legged kittiwake plots in the Chiswell Islands, AK.

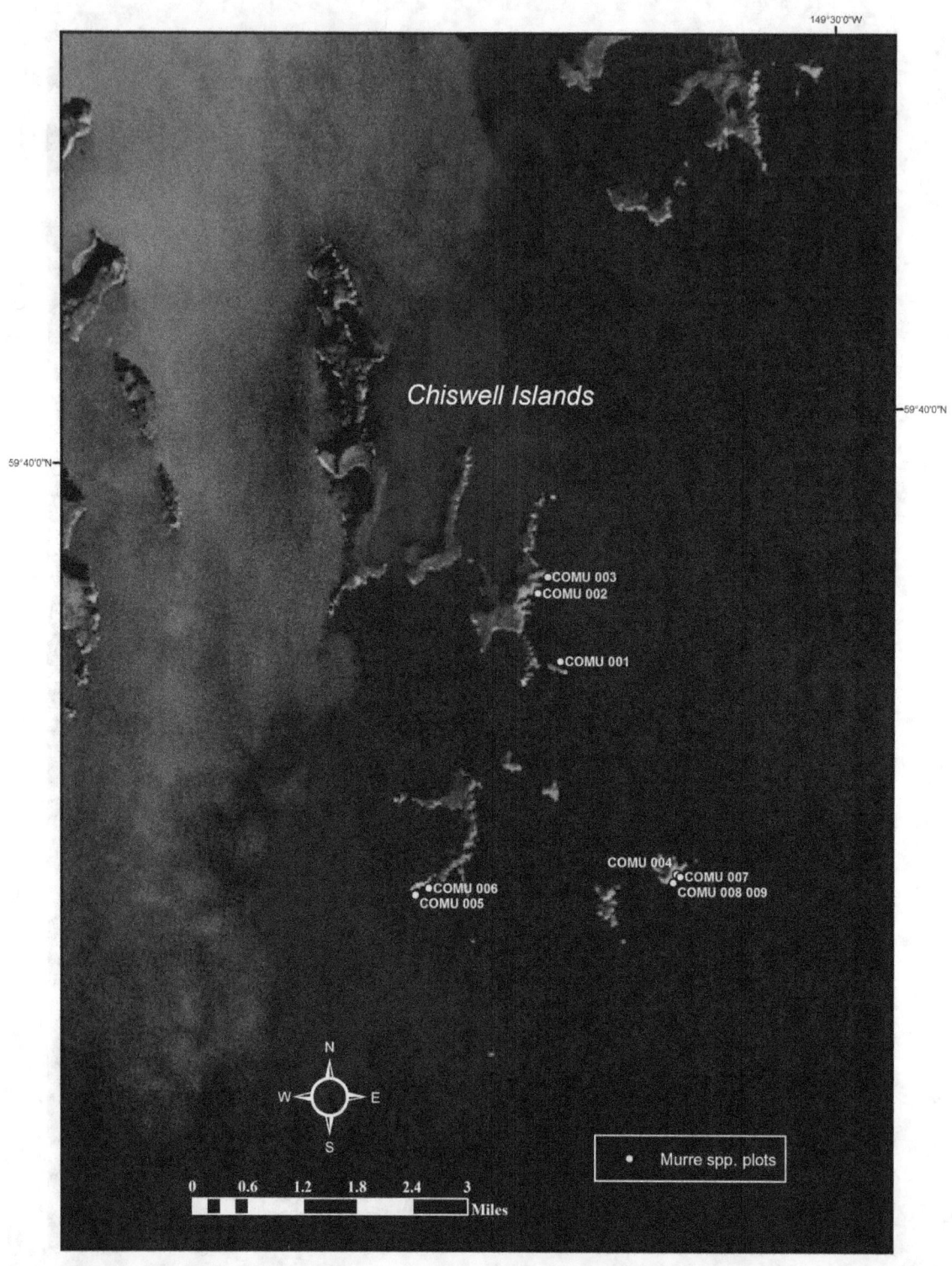

Figure 6. Locations of common murre plots in the Chiswell Islands, AK.

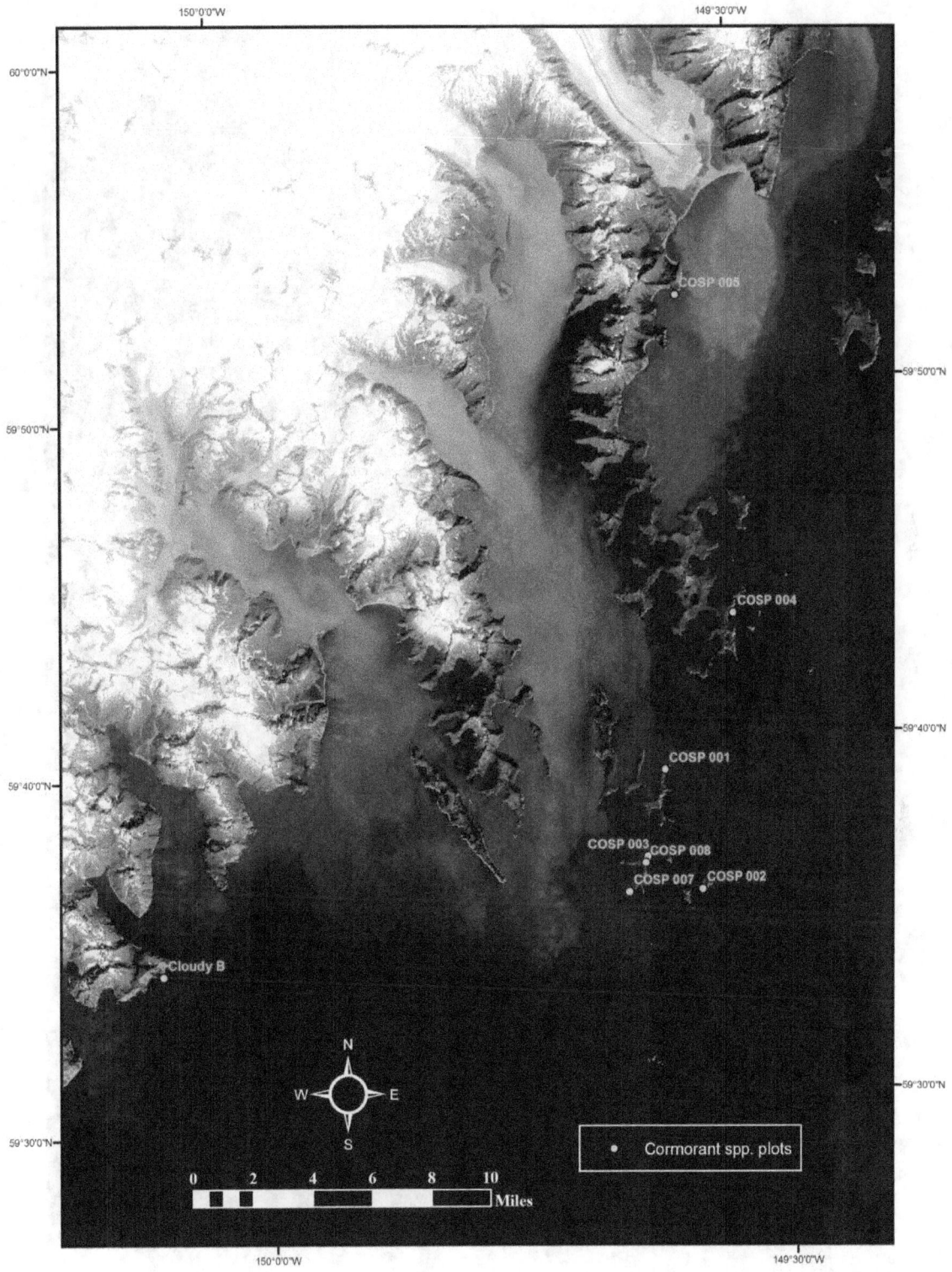

Figure 7. Locations of cormorant plots in Kenai Fjords National Park and Alaska Maritime National Wildlife Refuge.

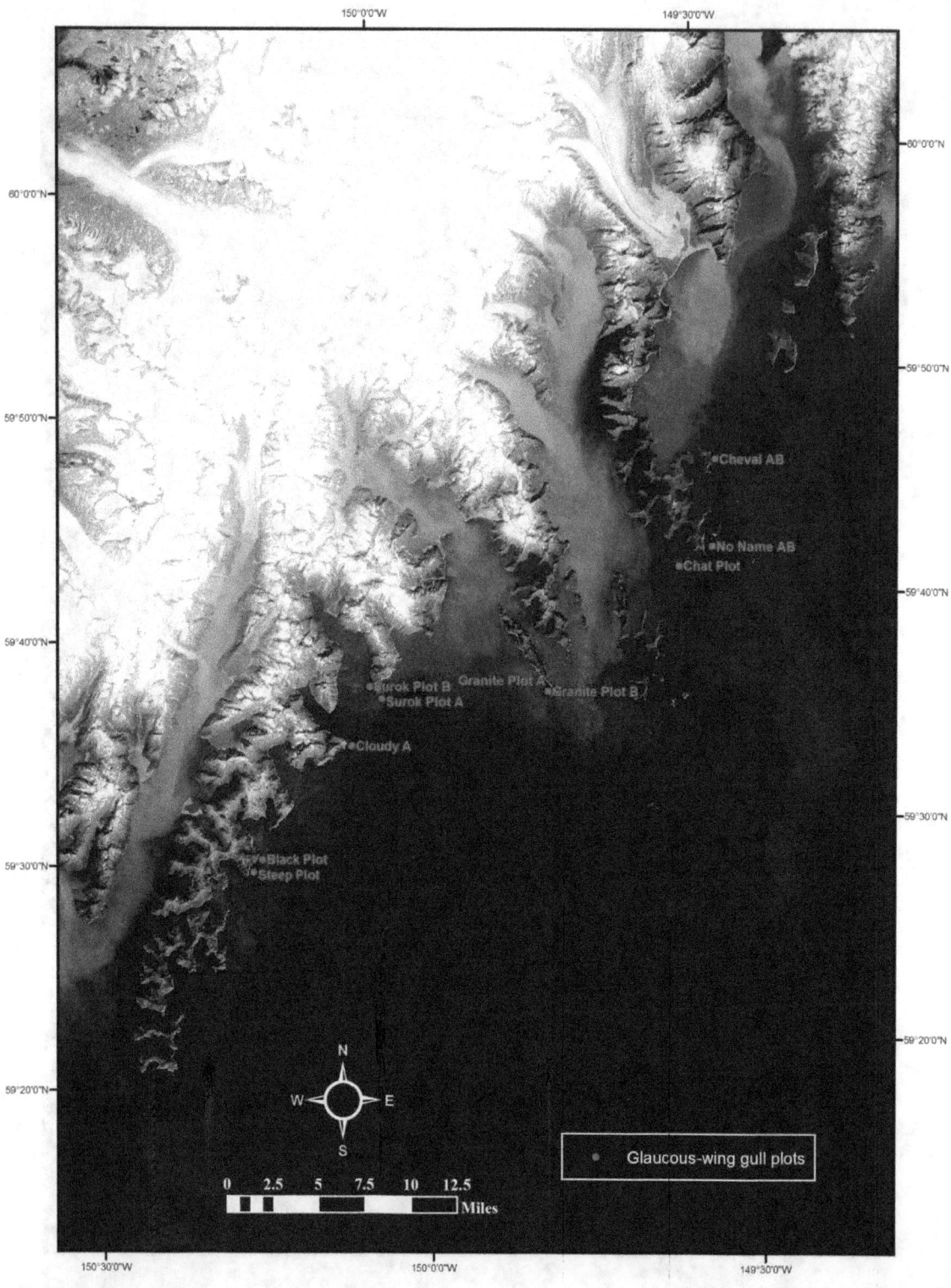

Figure 8. Locations of glaucous-winged gull plots in Kenai Fjords National Park and Alaska Maritime National Wildlife Refuge.

Results

Coastline Surveys

We located 35 known colony locations within KEFJ and AMNWR during coastline surveys, and discovered an additional 18 new colonies in 2011 (Figure 3, Figure 4). All but one of the newly discovered colonies were single species colonies (one mixed horned and tufted puffin, seven horned puffin, four cormorant, three mew gull, and three glaucous-winged gull colonies). We surveyed two locations (between Yalik Point and Beauty Bay and at Bear Point in Two Arm Bay) where groups of 8-12 horned puffins were observed on the water but not on land. We made a note of these locations but did not consider them new colonies since individuals were not observed on land. We were unable to detect any breeding activity at seven historic sites (Harrington Point, East Arm (James Lagoon), Northwestern Lagoon, Try Triangle, 17 Cove, East Aialik Peninsula and Harris Bay Island). Three of the seven unoccupied colony locations previously supported multiple breeding species (glaucous-winged gulls, mew gulls, arctic terns, red-faced, double-crested and pelagic cormorants, and horned puffins), the other four locations previously supported single species (three horned puffin colonies and one glaucous-winged gull colony) (Appendix A: Table 1, Table 2).

Whole Colony Counts

We revisited most colonies one to four times but completed seven to eight replicates at four colonies. Descriptive comparisons of limited count data available for select seabird species at colonies with multiple years of data reflect the apparent variability of colony attendance since 1976 (Appendix A: Table 1, Table 2). Generally, the number of breeding glaucous-winged gulls at colonies in KEFJ and AMNWR has increased since surveys in 1976 and 1986 (Figure 9, Figure 10). The number of breeding cormorants varied among years with higher numbers of birds attending colonies in 1976 and 2009 and much lower numbers in 2007 and 2011 (Figure 11, Figure 12). Apparent numbers of horned puffins have declined at four colonies (Granite Island, Black Bay, Hoof Point, and Bear Glacier Point), fluctuated or remained stable at four colonies (Aialik Cape, Cliff Bay, Surok Point and Spire Cove) and increased at one colony (Aligo Point) (Figure 13, Figure 14).

13

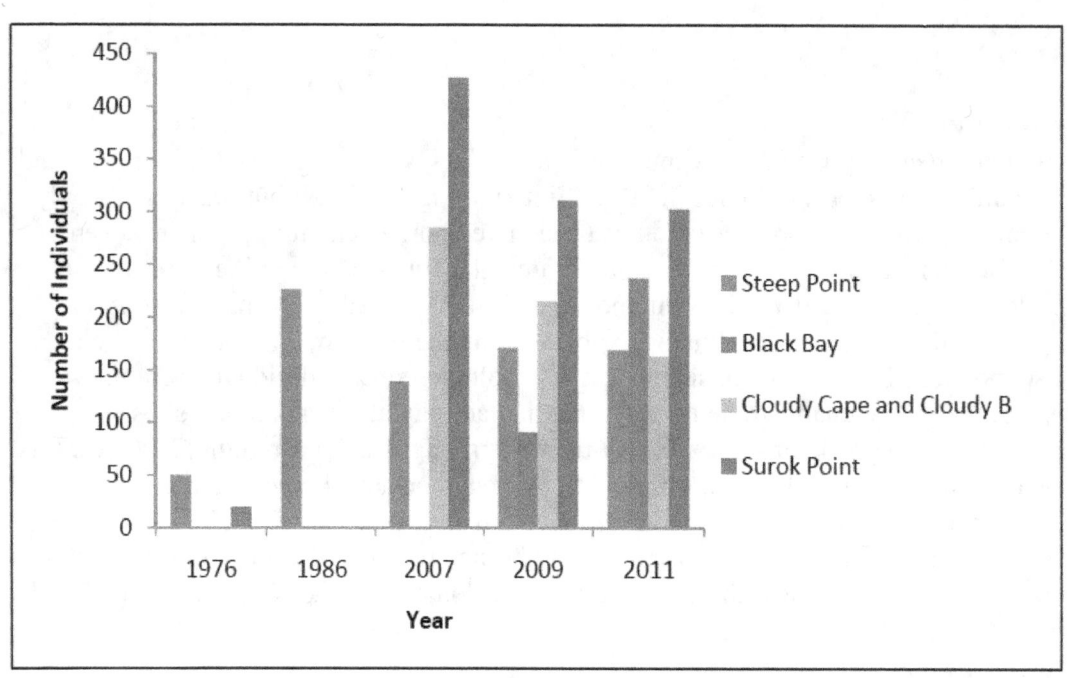

Figure 9. Apparent breeding population of glaucous-winged gulls at four colonies in KEFJ for five years of count data. Counts for 1976-2009 are from single visits. In 2011 counts are an average from multiple visits: Steep Point was visited two times, Black Bay three times, Cloudy Cape and Cloudy B nine times and Surok Point four times.

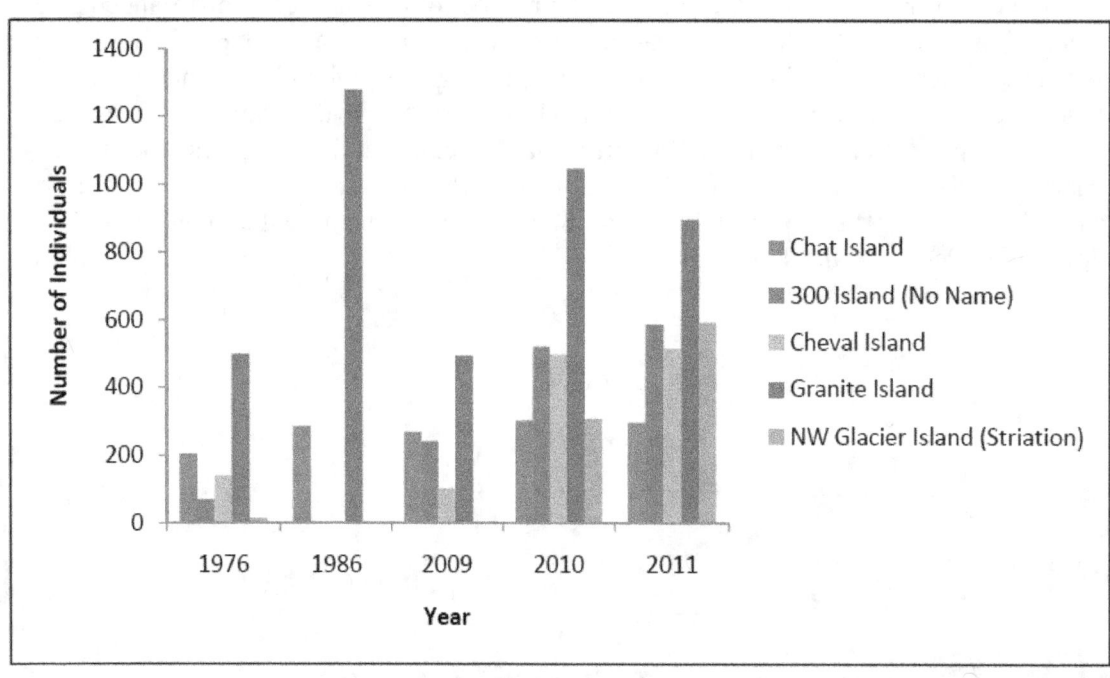

Figure 10. Apparent breeding population of glaucous-winged gulls at five colonies in AMNWR for five years of count data. All counts are from single visits.

14

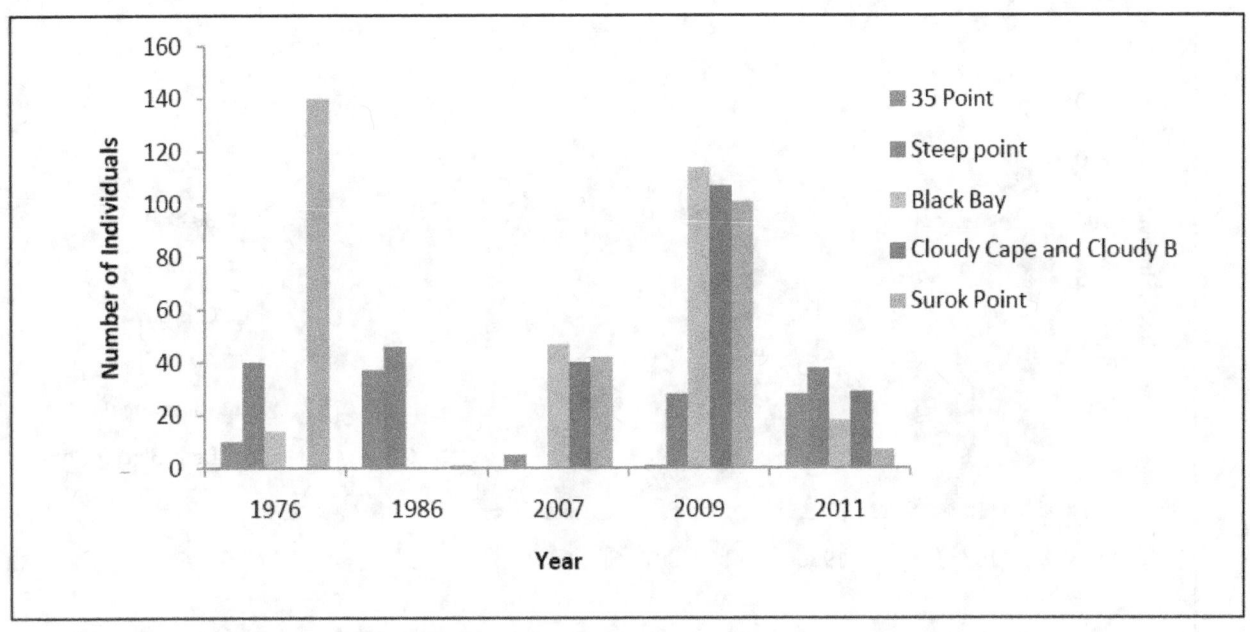

Figure 11. Apparent breeding population of three species of cormorant (red-faced, double-crested, and pelagic) at five colonies in KEFJ for five years of count data. Counts for 1976-2009 are from single visits. With the exception of 35 Point, 2011 counts are an average from multiple visits: Steep Point was visited two times, Black Bay three times, Cloudy Cape and Cloudy B nine times and Surok Point four times.

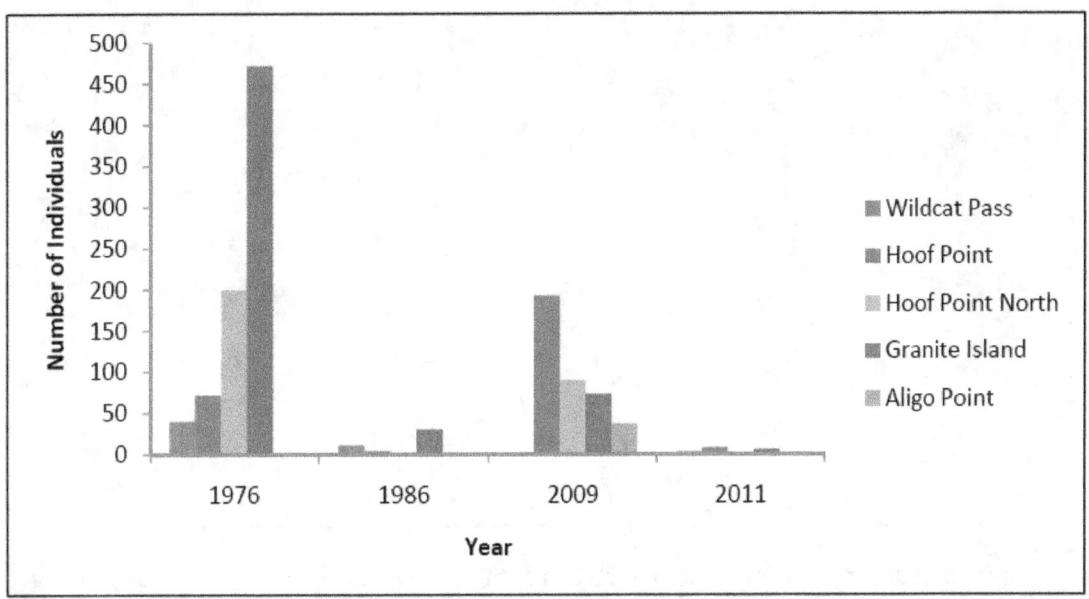

Figure 12. Apparent breeding population of three species of cormorant (red-faced, double-crested, and pelagic) at five colonies in AMNWR for four years of count data. All counts are from single visits.

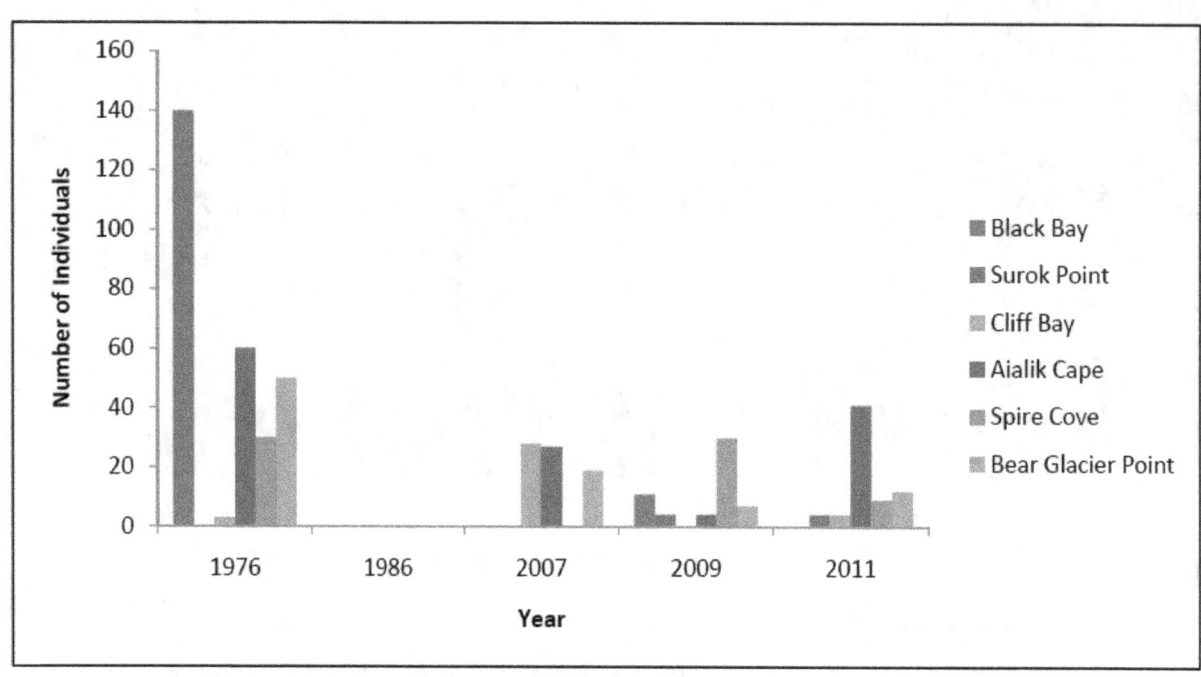

Figure 13. Apparent breeding population of horned puffins at six colonies in KEFJ for five years of count data. All but two counts are from single visits. Number of birds present at Black Bay and Surok Point in 2011 are the average of two visits.

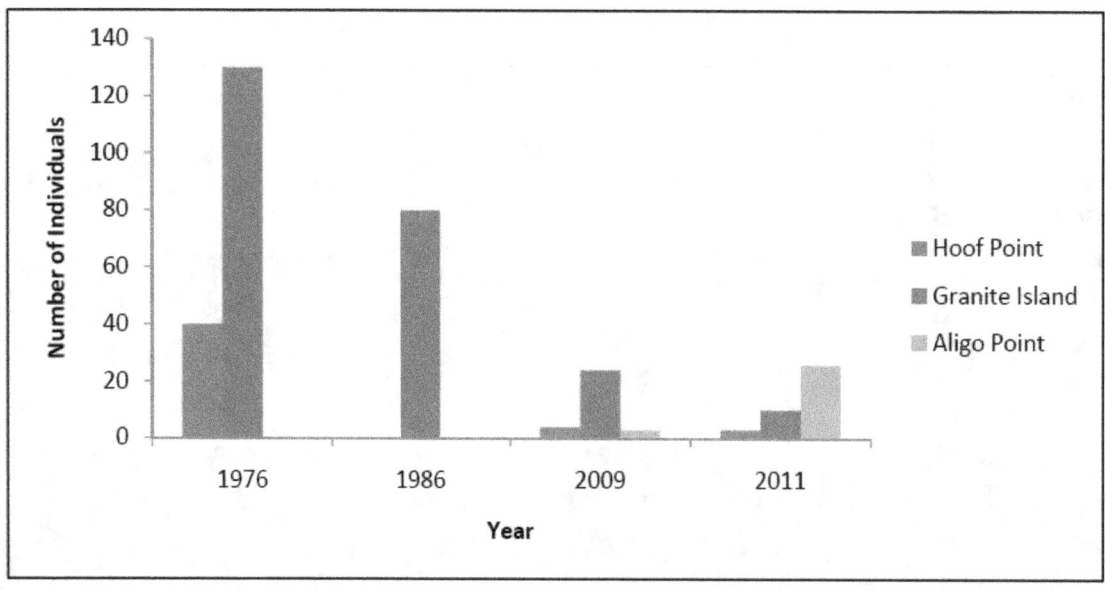

Figure 14. Apparent breeding population of horned puffins at three colonies in AMNWR for four years of count data. All counts are from single visits.

Plot Establishment and Counts

We revisited historic black-legged kittiwake plots in the Chiswell Islands ten times and revisited two new kittiwake plots on Matushka Island and Unnamed Chiswell A Island eight times (Appendix A: Table 3). The average numbers of birds and nests present in 2011 in the eight historic plots, when descriptively compared to data collected in 1992 and 2008, show that numbers varied among years and plots, with the number of birds decreasing in some plots and increasing in others (Figure 15). The total sum of birds present among all plots decreased between 2008 and 2011 but both 2008 and 2011 had more birds and nests than 1992 (Figure 16).

Nine common murre plots were established in the Chiswell Islands and were counted eight to ten times. The number of murres present on plots was highly variable among days (Appendix A: Table 4).

Three cormorant plots (004, 005 and Cloudy B) were established on the mainland in KEFJ and six were established in the Chiswell Islands. Species composition of cormorant plots varied with one to two species of cormorant present in each. Red-faced cormorants were only present in one plot in 2011. Numbers of pelagic cormorants nesting in plots declined steadily over the course of the summer (Appendix A: Table 5). Double crested cormorant numbers were more stable except at Cloudy B where they declined three-fold between the first week of July and the first week of August (Appendix A: Table 6).

We established twelve glaucous-winged gull plots, five in KEFJ and seven on AMNWR islands (Figure 8). Plots were counted six to nine times during July and early August (Appendix A: Table 7). Number of gulls present in plots varied greatly among days but did not exhibit a trend over the course of the summer.

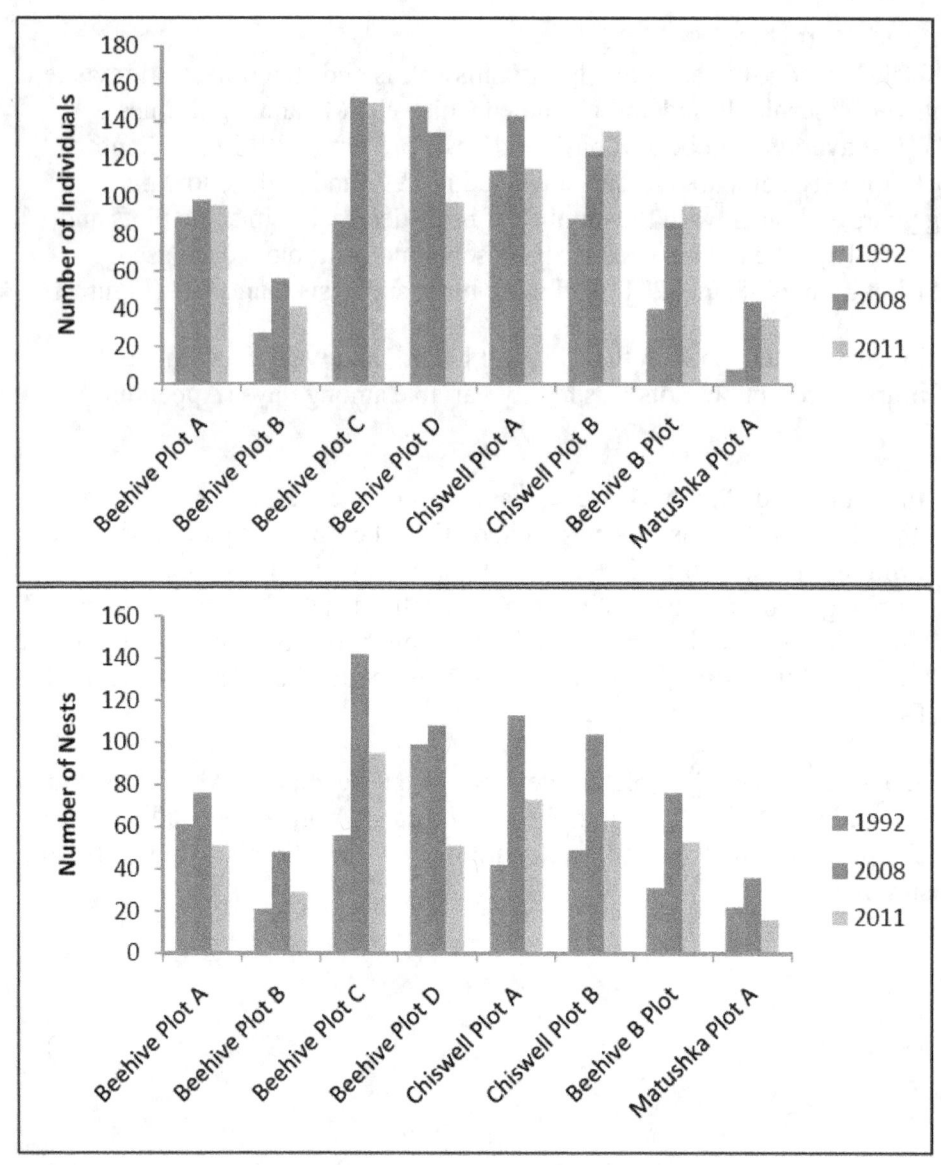

Figure 15. Number of adult black-legged kittiwakes (top) and nests (bottom) for eight historic kittiwake plots in the Chiswell Islands, AK. Counts from 1993 are the average count for three visits, counts from 2008 are from a single visit and counts from 2011 are the average from ten visits.

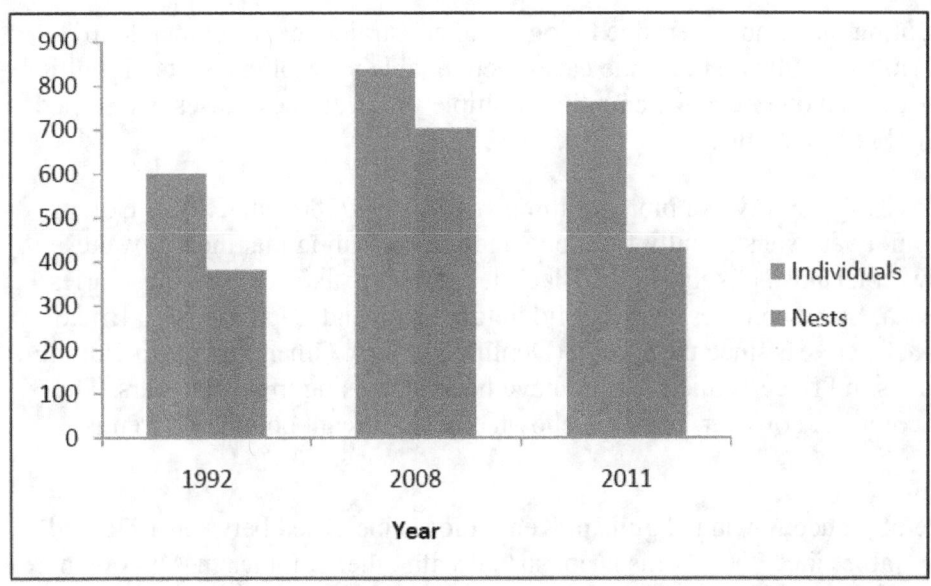

Figure 16. Total number of adult black-legged kittiwake adults and nests present within the boundaries of eight historic kittiwake plots in the Chiswell Islands, AK for three survey years (1992, 2008, 2011).

Discussion

Seabird colony surveys have been conducted along the eastern Kenai Peninsula only sporadically since 1976. During past survey efforts, replicate counts were rarely made and direct comparisons of data to recent surveys are complicated by differing survey techniques and record keeping. When Bailey (1977) conducted his surveys of seabird colonies along the Kenai Fjords coastline, he made single counts of adult ledge-nesting seabirds (gulls, murres, cormorants and kittiwakes) at small cliffs, but frequently estimated numbers of birds at larger colonies by extrapolating from counts on portions of the cliff. He estimated populations of tufted puffins by enumerating and extrapolating burrows and individuals visible during boat based surveys and horned puffins from observed numbers and the amount of suitable habitat available. His estimates of puffin numbers are higher than any obtained on subsequent surveys in the Kenai Fjords area possibly due to his estimation methods; however, none of the surveys conducted since have used robust survey techniques for monitoring puffin numbers, especially tufted puffins (USFWS 2000b).

While Nishimoto and Rice (1987) attempted to duplicate Bailey's (1977) survey techniques to facilitate comparisons, a number of differences in methods and reporting make comparisons difficult. Nishimoto and Rice generally surveyed off a small inflatable boat resulting in a more limited field of view than Bailey (1977). Nishimoto and Rice also reported many colony counts by area, lumping observations from multiple colonies into area totals or birds off colony (on water or in air) on transects in count totals making it difficult to compare across years at specific sites. They also appeared constrained in their survey schedule, suggesting that counts in some areas may have been artificially lower or absent due to lack of time.

Recent surveys conducted by NPS and USFWS since 2007 were generally performed from a larger vessel and observers made duplicate counts of birds on a single visit at most colonies visited. In 2011 we were able to follow USFWS protocols for estimating relative abundance of ledge-nesting species (USFWS 2000a). We attempted to follow USFWS protocols for population trend indices when counting plots; however, due to logistical constraints we were unable to restrict our counts to 11:00 – 18:00h and in some cases were unable to resolve counts of multiple observers to within 5% of each other despite counting multiple times. In these cases, we settled for two counts within 10% of each other.

We have counts of black-legged kittiwake plots for three years: 1992, 2008, and 2011. Counts for these three years do not vary substantially from one another indicating that the kittiwake population in the Chiswell Islands is likely stable. Black-legged kittiwake colony status varies widely throughout Alaska. Some colonies such as Middleton Island and Cape Pierce in Bristol Bay have decreased 6-8% per year since the 1990's (Denlinger 2006). Other colonies including Buldir Island and colonies in Prince William Sound have been increasing in recent years. The majority of monitored colonies, however, have not shown any significant population trends (USFWS 2006).

The relative abundance of glaucous-winged gulls in Kenai Fjords increased between 1976 and 2007 but has remained stable since 2007. This is consistent with other colonies in Alaska where gull colonies are currently stable, and Middleton Island where gull numbers increased from the mid-1980s to the mid-1990s but are now declining (USFWS 2006). Growth of glaucous-winged gull colonies in the 20th century is often attributed to increases in gull use of anthropogenic food sources including open refuse dumps and fish waste discarded from fishing vessels (Denlinger 2006). While these sources are still used by gulls, the recent stabilization and even decline of some colonies has been attributed to increased predation pressure by bald eagles (Sullivan et al. 2002 and Hayward et al. 2010).

Cormorant breeding in Kenai Fjords is highly variable. 1976 and 2009 appear to have been years of high breeding effort while 1986, 2007 and 2011 had lower breeding effort. In 2011 we noted that the numbers of pelagic cormorant nests on plots decreased as the season progressed. Pelagic cormorant populations are generally stable at most monitored sites in Alaska. In contrast, red-faced cormorant populations in the Aleutian Islands are decreasing while populations in the Gulf of Alaska are increasing (USFWS 2006). Double-crested cormorants are not well studied in Alaska and population trends are unknown.

The decline in the number of horned puffins nesting in our study area may be due to differences in census techniques between 1976 and 2007-2011; however, at sea surveys in Prince William Sound have documented a 79% decline in the number of horned puffins observed from 1972 to 1998 which is consistent with the apparent decline in Kenai Fjords (USFWS 2006). Changes in the marine climate in the last 30 years have resulted in changes in the prey base of fish eating seabirds and may be playing a role in puffin declines (USFWS 2006).

Colony locations can be fairly stable for many species; however, others, most notably cormorants, move colonies frequently (USFWS 2006). Using GIS coordinates has improved our ability to accurately identify colony locations, although time of day, season and weather during which the surveys are performed might affect the ability to identify locations and may affect the number of individuals observed at colonies. Shifting of individuals from one colony to another among years may also affect count estimates for populations if the area surveyed does not adequately monitor potential breeding habitat. The discovery of 18 new breeding sites in 2011 and the lack of breeding at seven historic sites illustrate the ephemeral nature of some seabird colonies.

Data gathered in 2011 will be complimented by intensive survey efforts next year. In 2012, we plan on experimenting with different techniques for conducting counts using photos, observer counts, and possibly aircraft. Data from these two years will be used to develop statistically valid protocols for monitoring ledge-nesting seabird populations and recommend long term monitoring strategies for seabirds nesting in the Kenai Fjords area.

Literature Cited

Alaska National Interest Lands Conservation Act. Pub. L. no. 96-487, 94 Stat 2371 (1980). Print

Bailey, E. P. 1977. Distribution and abundance of marine birds and mammals along the south side of the Kenai Peninsula, Alaska. Murrelet 58:58-72.

Denlinger, L. M. 2006. Alaska Seabird Information Series. Unpublished report. USFWS Migratory Bird Management, Nongame Program, Anchorage, AK.

Dragoo, D. E. 1994. Counts of black-legged kittiwakes at the Chiswell and Barren Islands, Alaska, in 1992. U.S. Fish and Wildlife Service Report, AMNWR 94/04. Homer, Alaska. 12pp.

Giffen, B., D. K. Hall, J. Y. L. Chien. Chapter 12 (2009): Alaska: Glaciers of Kenai Fjords National Park and Katmai National Park and Preserve. *In* Global Land Ice Measurements from Space.

Hahr, M. 2009. 2008 Seabird Colony Survey Trip Report: Kenai Fjords National Park and Alaska Maritime National Wildlife Refuge. Kenai Fjords National Park, U.S.D.I. National Park Service, Seward, AK. 11pp.

Hahr, M. 2008. Seabird Colony Survey Trip Report 2007: Kenai Fjords National Park. Kenai Fjords National Park, U.S.D.I. National Park Service, Seward, AK. 15 pp.

Hayward, J. L., J. G. Galusha, and S. M. Henson. 2010. Foraging-related activity of bald eagles at a Washington seabird colony and seal rookery. Journal of Raptor Research 44: 19-29.

Lindsay, C. and F. Klasner. 2009. Annual Climate Summary for 2007-2008: Kenai Fjords National Park. Kenai Fjords National Park, U.S.D.I. National Park Service, Seward, AK. 32 pp.

McFarland, B., S. Hall, and L. Slater. 2009. Seabird Colony Trip Report: Kenai Fjords National Park and Alaska Maritime National Wildlife Refuge. Kenai Fjords National Park, U.S. Department of Interior, National Park Service, Seward, AK.

Nishimoto, M. and B. Rice. 1987. A Re-survey of seabirds and marine mammals along the south coast of the Kenai Peninsula, Alaska during the summer of 1986. Unpublished report, Cooperative Research Project, U.S. Fish and Wildlife Service, National Park Service, Anchorage, Alaska.

Nysewander, D. R., C. H. Dippel, G.V. Byrd, and E. P. Knudtson. 1993. Effects of the *Exxon Valdez* oil spill on murres: a perspective from observation at breeding colonies. *Exxon Valdez* Oil Spill State/Federal Natural Resource Damage Assessment Final Report (Bird Study Number 3), U.S. Fish and Wildlife Service, homer, Alaska.

Phillips, L. and B. McFarland. 2010. Seabird Colony Survey Report 2010: Kenai Fjords National Park and Alaska Maritime National Wildlife Refuge. Kenai Fjords National Park, U.S. Department of Interior, National Park Service, Seward, AK.

Piatt, J., W. J. Sydeman, and F. Wiese. 2007. Introduction: A modern role of seabirds as indicators. Marine Ecology Progress Series. 352:199-204.

Sullivan, T. M., S. L. Hazlitt, and M. J. F. Lemon. 2002. Population trends of nesting glaucous-winged gulls, *Larus glaucescens*, in the Southern Strait of Georgia, British Columbia. Canadian Field-Naturalist 116: 603-606.

U. S. D. I. 2006. General Agreement among the National Oceanic and Atmospheric Administration, U.S. Department of Commerce, U.S. Fish and Wildlife Service, and National Park Service. MOA-2006-036/7196.

USFWS. 2000a. Standard operating procedures for monitoring populations and productivity: ledge-nesting seabirds. U.S. Fish and Wildl. Serv. Rep., Homer, Alaska.

USFWS. 2000b. Standard operating procedures for population inventories: Burrow-nesting seabirds. U.S. Fish and Wildl. Serv. Rep., Homer, Alaska.

USFWS. 2000c. Standard operating procedures for population inventories: Crevice-nesting seabirds. U.S. Fish and Wildl. Serv. Rep., Homer, Alaska.

USFWS 1998. Alaska seabird colony catalog: suggestions for censusing seabird colonies and reporting data. U.S. Fish and Wildlife Service, Migratory Bird Management, Anchorage, Alaska.

Wittenberger, J. F. and G. L. Hunt Jr. 1985. The adaptive significance of coloniality in birds. *In* D. S. Farner, J. R. King, and K. C. Parkes (eds). Avian Biology, vol. VIII: 1-78. Academic Press, London.

Appendix A: Summary Tables

Table 1. Species composition and abundance at seabird colonies in KEFJ for all surveys, 1976-2011. Colony survey locations are listed west to east, from Nuka Bay to Resurrection Bay. * Denotes lack of data for a site/year combination, - indicates no sightings for that category.

Colony/Spp	1976	1986	2007	2008	2009	2010	2011
35 Point							
Glaucous-winged gull	30	-	95	*	90	*	33
Red-faced cormorant	10	-	-	*	-	*	27
Nests	-	-	-	*	-	*	2
Double-crested cormorant	-	12	5	*	-	*	-
Nests	-	3	-	*	-	*	-
Pelagic cormorant	-	25	-	*	1	*	1
Nests	-	1	-	*	-	*	0
Cormorant sp.	-	-	-	*	-	*	-
Nests	-	-	10	*	-	*	-
Harrington Point							
Glaucous-winged gull	-	-	166	*	1	*	-
Red-faced cormorant	-	29	-	*	-	*	-
Nests	-	21	-	*	-	*	-
Double-crested cormorant	-	-	18	*	-	*	-
Nests	-	-	5	*	-	*	-
Pelagic cormorant	-	12	-	*	-	*	-
Nests	-	17	-	*	-	*	-
Horned puffin	10	-	-	*	-	*	-
Harrington Point West							
Glaucous-winged gull	-	85	-	*	4	*	50
Red-faced cormorant	-	-	-	*	-	*	5
Nests	-	-	-	*	-	*	0
Double-crested cormorant	-	-	-	*	41	*	32
Nests	-	-	-	*	64	*	21
Pelagic cormorant	20	-	-	*	-	*	15
Nests	-	-	-	*	-	*	5
East Arm (James Lagoon)							
Glaucous-winged gull	120	-	-	*	-	*	-
East Arm North							
Arctic Tern	6	-	-	*	-	*	-
Glaucous-winged gull	40	162	-	*	4	*	7

Table 2. Species composition and abundance at seabird colonies in KEFJ for all surveys, 1976-2011. Colony survey locations are listed west to east, from Nuka Bay to Resurrection Bay (continued).

Colony/Spp	1976	1986	2007	2008	2009	2010	2011
McCarty Fjord							
Mew gull	*	*	*	*	*	*	9
Delusion							
Mew gull	*	*	*	*	*	*	18
Chance Cove							
Horned puffin	*	*	*	*	*	*	8
Steep Point							
Glaucous-winged gulls	50	226	139	*	171	*	169[1]
Red-faced cormorant	-	-	-	*	-	*	19[1]
Nests	-	-	-	*	-	*	0[1]
Double-crested cormorants	-	-	-	*	1	*	-
Pelagic cormorants	40	46	-	*	27	*	11[1]
Nests	-	2	-	*	12	*	6[1]
Tufted puffin	-	-	-	*	11	*	-
Cormorant Spp	-	-	-	*	-	*	8[1]
Nests	-	-	-	*	-	*	5[1]
Black Bay							
Glaucous-winged gull	-	-	-	*	91	*	237[2]
Red-faced cormorant	-	-	-	*	14	*	4[2]
Nests	-	-	-	*	11	*	0[2]
Double-crested cormorant	-	-	20	*	69	*	-
Nests	-	-	12	*	42	*	-
Pelagic cormorant	14	-	27	*	31	*	11[2]
Nests	60	-	21	*	22	*	8[2]
Cormorant Spp	-	-	-	*	-	*	3[2]
Nests	-	-	-	*	-	*	3[2]
Horned puffin	140	-	-	*	11	*	-
Tufted puffin	-	-	1	*	16	*	2[2]
Common murre	-	-	3	*	11	*	-
Thunder Bay East							
Glaucous-winged Gull	*	*	*	*	*	*	9

Table 3. Species composition and abundance at seabird colonies in KEFJ for all surveys, 1976-2011. Colony survey locations are listed west to east, from Nuka Bay to Resurrection Bay (continued).

Colony/Spp	1976	1986	2007	2008	2009	2010	2011
Thunder Bay East B							
Pelagic Cormorant	*	*	*	*	*	*	2
Nests	*	*	*	*	*	*	2
Nack Triangle							
Glaucous-winged gull	-	-	-	*	11	*	-
Red-faced cormorant	40	-	-	*	3	*	9
Nests	-	-	-	*	*	*	0
Black-legged kittiwake	-	-	-	*	-	*	0
Nests	-	62	-	*	-	*	0
Pelagic cormorant	20	-	-	*	-	*	23
Nests	-	-	-	*	-	*	9
Nack Triangle B							
Pelagic cormorant	*	*	*	*	*	*	11
Nests	*	*	*	*	*	*	9
Cloudy Cape							
Glaucous-winged gull	-	-	285	*	215^3	*	163^4
Black-legged kittiwake	-	22	-	*	-	*	-
Red-faced cormorant	-	-	-	*	2^3	*	-
Double-crested cormorant	-	-	40	*	35^3	*	-
Nests	-	-	27	*	26^3	*	-
Pelagic cormorant	-	-	-	*	70^3	*	1^2
Nests	-	-	-	*	24^3	*	1^2
Cormorant *sp.*	-	-	-	*	-	*	-
Nests	-	-	-	*	7^3	*	-
Horned puffin	-	-	-	*	2^3	*	5
Tufted puffin	-	-	-	*	7^3	*	9
Cloudy B							
Glaucous-winged gull	*	*	*	*	215^3	*	-
Red-faced cormorant	*	*	*	*	2^3	*	-
Double-crested cormorant	*	*	*	*	35^3	*	23^4
Nests	*	*	*	*	26^3	*	21^4
Pelagic cormorant	*	*	*	*	70^3	*	5^5
Nests	*	*	*	*	24^3	*	5^5
Cormorant *sp.*	*	*	*	*	-	*	-
Nests	*	*	*	*	7^3	*	-

Table 4. Species composition and abundance at seabird colonies in KEFJ for all surveys, 1976-2011. Colony survey locations are listed west to east, from Nuka Bay to Resurrection Bay (continued).

Colony/Spp	1976	1986	2007	2008	2009	2010	2011
Cloudy B							
Horned puffin	*	*	*	*	2[3]	*	-
Tufted puffin	*	*	*	*	7[3]	*	3[1]
Surok Point							
Glaucous-winged gulls	20	-	427	*	311	*	303[6]
Red-faced cormorant	-	-	-	*	2	*	2
Nests	-	-	-	*	1	*	-
Double-crested cormorant	-	-	9	*	27	*	2[6]
Nests	-	-	9	*	6	*	1[6]
Pelagic cormorant	140	1	33	*	72	*	3[6]
Nests	-	1	33	*	55	*	2[6]
Tufted puffin	-	-	-	*	15	*	5
Horned puffin	-	-	-	*	4	*	4[1]
Surok B							
Pelagic cormorant	*	*	*	*	*	*	5
Nests	*	*	*	*	*	*	1
Sandy Bay							
Horned puffin	*	*	*	*	*	*	3
Tufted puffin	*	*	*	*	*	*	2
Northwestern Lagoon							
Arctic tern	150	-	-	*	*	*	-
Glaucous-winged gulls	170	-	-	*	*	*	-
Mew gull	90	-	-	*	*	*	-
NW Glacier							
Glaucous-winged gulls	*	*	*	*	*	82	180
NW Glacier B							
Glaucous-winged gulls	*	*	*	*	*	*	32
Try Triangle							
Horned puffin	10	-	-	*	-	*	-
17 Cove							
Horned puffin	10	-	-	*	-	*	-

Table 5. Species composition and abundance at seabird colonies in KEFJ for all surveys, 1976-2011. Colony survey locations are listed west to east, from Nuka Bay to Resurrection Bay (continued).

Colony/Spp	1976	1986	2007	2008	2009	2010	2011
Cliff Bay							
Double-crested cormorant	-	-	30	*	-	-	-
Pelagic cormorant	-	-	17	*	-	11	4
Horned puffin	3	-	28	*	-	-	4
Aialik Cape							
Glacous-winged gull	-	-	-	98	-	-	-
Black-legged kittiwake	-	-	-	3	-	-	-
Red-faced cormorant	-	74[7]	-	-	99	51	-
Nests	-	43[7]	-	-	72	*	-
Double-crested cormorant	-	-	-	9	66	26	23[5]
Nests	-	-	-	(2 chicks)	40	*	20[5]
Pelagic cormorant	-	63[7]	-	22	66	104	-
Nests	-	23[7]	-	(6 chicks)	47	*	-
Cormorant sp.	-	8[7]	-	-	2	-	-
Nests	-	12[7]	-	-	7	-	-
Horned puffin	60	-	27	9	4	10	41
Tufted puffin	-	-	-	17	6	-	-
East Aialik Peninsula							
Horned puffin	20	-	-	*	12	*	-
Cheval Narrows							
Horned puffin	*	*	*	*	*	*	16
Porcupine Cove							
Horned puffin	*	*	*	*	*	*	8
Spire Cove C							
Horned puffin	*	*	*	*	*	*	5
Spire Cove B							
Horned puffin	*	*	*	*	*	*	3

Table 6. Species composition and abundance at seabird colonies in KEFJ for all surveys, 1976-2011. Colony survey locations are listed west to east, from Nuka Bay to Resurrection Bay (continued).

Colony/Spp	1976	1986	2007	2008	2009	2010	2011
Spire Cove							
Red-faced Cormorant	-	-	-	*	-	-	3[8]
Nests	-	-	-	*	-	-	1[8]
Pelagic cormorant	-	-	-	*	11	-	10[8]
Nests	-	-	-	*	2	-	6[8]
Cormorant sp.	-	-	-	*	-	15	-
Nests	-	-	-	*	-	*	-
Horned puffin	30	-	-	*	30	1	9
Bear Glacier Point B							
Horned puffin	*	*	*	*	*	*	2
Bear Glacier Point							
Glacous-winged gull	-	-	-	32	-	*	-
Black-legged kittiwake	-	-	-	23	-	*	-
Double-crested cormorant	-	-	-	7	-	*	-
Nests	-	-	-	(8 chicks)	-	*	-
Pelagic cormorant	-	-	12	14	-	*	-
Nests	-	-	6	(2 chicks)	-	*	-
Horned puffin	50	-	19	4	7	*	12
Bulldog Cove							
Horned puffin	*	*	*	*	*	*	4

[1] Average of counts from two visits

[2] Average of counts from three visits
[3] Cloudy Cape and Cloudy B colonies are combined in the 2009 survey data.
[4] Average of counts from nine visits

[5] Average of counts from seven visits

[6] Average of counts from four visits

[7] 300 Island (No Name) and Aialik Cape colonies are combined in the 1986 survey data.
[8] Average of counts from eight visits

Table 7. Species composition and abundance at seabird colonies in AMNWR for all surveys, 1976-2011. Colony survey locations are listed west to east, from Nuka Bay to Resurrection Bay. * Denotes a lack of data for a site/year combination, - indicates no sightings for that category.

Colony/Spp	1976	1986	2007	2009	2010	2011
Outer Island S to SE						
Glaucous-winged gull	190	1022	*	417	*	*
Red-faced cormorant	30	-	*	-	*	*
Pelagic cormorant	40	10	*	-	*	*
Cormorant sp.	-	-	*	15	*	*
Horned puffin	-	25	*	2	*	*
Tufted puffin	180	648	*	31	*	*
Common murre	-	2	*	-	*	*
Outer Island Southeast						*
Glaucous-winged gull	100	556	*	505	*	*
Black-legged kittiwake	1060	1089	*	759	*	*
Nests	*	501	*	70	*	*
Red-faced cormorant	20	36	*	-	*	*
Nests	*	9	*	-	*	*
Pelagic cormorant	80	28	*	26	*	*
Nests	*	12	*	-	*	*
Cormorant sp.	-	-	*	2	*	*
Horned puffin	100	30	*	10	*	*
Tufted puffin	500	58	*	109	*	*
Rabbit Island						
Pelagic cormorant	4	-	*	-	*	*
Cormorant sp.	-	-	*	72	*	*
Horned puffin	30	-	*	-	*	*
Wildcat Pass						
Glaucous-winged gull	-	4	*	242	*	22
Pelagic cormorant	40	11	*	-	*	3
Nests	*	*	*	-	*	2
Horned puffin	30	-	*	-	*	-
Tufted puffin	30	-	*	-	*	-
Hoof Point						
Glaucous-winged gull	90	137	*	297	*	403[1]
Black-legged kittiwake	-	59	*	68	*	-
Red-faced cormorant	60	-	*	-	*	-
Double-crested cormorant	-	-	*	28	*	-
Nests	-	-	*	16	*	-

Table 8. Species composition and abundance at seabird colonies in AMNWR for all surveys, 1976-2011. Colony survey locations are listed west to east, from Nuka Bay to Resurrection Bay. (continued)

Colony/Spp	1976	1986	2007	2009	2010	2011
Hoof Point						
Pelagic cormorant	12	4	*	165	*	-
Nests	-	-	*	29	*	-
Cormorant sp.	-	-	*	-	*	8
Nests	-	-	*	2	*	4
Horned puffin	40	-	*	4	*	3
Tufted puffin	20	-	*	7	*	-
Hoof Point North						
Glaucous-winged gull	80	-	*	731	*	353[1]
Red-faced cormorant	40	-	*	-	*	-
Nests	*	18	*	-	*	-
Double-crested cormorant	-	-	*	4	*	-
Nests	-	-	*	1	*	-
Pelagic cormorant	160	-	*	86	*	-
Nests	*	48	*	26	*	-
Cormorant sp.	-	-	*	-	*	-
Nests	-	-	*	7	*	-
Horned puffin	1000	-	*	8	*	1
Tufted puffin	800	-	*	14	*	-
28 Section						
Glaucous-winged gull	-	-	*	58	*	51[1]
Double-crested cormorant	-	-	*	124	*	-
Nests	-	-	*	100	*	-
Pelagic cormorant	10	present	*	33	*	-
Nests	-	-	*	23	*	-
Cormorant sp.	-	-	*	-	*	-
Nests	-	-	*	19	*	-
Tufted puffin	150	-	*	17	*	1
28 Section West						
Cormorant sp.	*	*	*	*	*	19
Nests	*	*	*	*	*	4
NW Glacier Island (Striation)						
Glaucous-winged gulls	16	-	-	309	594	691
Harris Bay Island (Erratic)						
Arctic tern	80	present	-	-	*	-
Glaucous-winged gull	40	-	-	30	*	-
Mew gull	60	present	-	-	*	-

Table 9. Species composition and abundance at seabird colonies in AMNWR for all surveys, 1976-2011. Colony survey locations are listed west to east, from Nuka Bay to Resurrection Bay. (continued)

Colony/Spp	1976	1986	2007	2009	2010	2011
Granite Island						
Glaucous-winged gull	500	1280	*	495	1048	897
Black-legged kittiwake	100	43	*	-	-	-
Red-faced cormorant	400	-	*	-	17	-
Double-crested cormorant	-	-	*	32	-	1
Nests	-	-	*	17	-	0
Pelagic cormorant	72	29	*	40	167	5
Nests	*	4	*	29	*	2
Cormorant sp.	-	1	*	1	-	-
Nests	-	-	*	25	-	-
Horned puffin	130	80	*	24	-	10
Tufted puffin	100	14	*	26	-	11
Common murre	200	18	*	55	77	90
Twin Islands						
Glaucous-winged gull	-	284	*	-	*	*
Black-legged kittiwake	-	22	*	-	*	*
Double-crested cormorant	-	5	*	-	*	*
Cormorant sp.	-	1	*	-	*	*
Horned puffin	50	122	*	35	*	*
Tufted puffin	-	3	*	-	*	*
Common murre	-	3	*	-	*	*
Aligo Point						
Red-faced cormorant	-	-	-	9	*	-
Nests	-	-	-	1	*	-
Double-crested cormorant	-	-	23	-	*	-
Pelagic cormorant	-	-	14	21	*	1
Nests	-	-	-	8	*	-
Cormorant sp.	-	-	-	-	*	-
Nests	-	3	-	4	*	-
Horned puffin	-	-	22	3	*	26
Puffin sp.	-	-	-	1	*	-
Slate Island						
Glaucous-winged gull	-	-	-	21	-	-
Mew gull	30	-	-	-	-	6
Nests	*	-	-	-	-	4
Horned puffin	56	-	-	1	-	-
Arctic tern	-	-	-	-	-	1

Table 10. Species composition and abundance at seabird colonies in AMNWR for all surveys, 1976-2011. Colony survey locations are listed west to east, from Nuka Bay to Resurrection Bay. (continued)

Colony/Spp	1976	1986	2007	2009	2010	2011
Squab Island						
Glaucous-winged gull	400	-	-	610	412	492
Abra						
Mew Gull	*	*	*	*	*	16
Nests	*	*	*	*	*	5
Chat Island						
Glaucous-winged gull	205	286	*	270	303	298
Red-faced cormorant	34	-	*	-	-	*
Double-crested cormorant	-	17	*	9	-	*
Nests	-	-	*	4	-	*
Pelagic cormorant	43	7	*	24	-	present
Nests	-	1	*	4	-	present
Cormorant sp.	-	1	*	-	29	present
Nests	-	-	*	2	-	present
Horned puffin	80	76	*	24	17	present
Tufted puffin	30	70	*	2	29	*
Common murre	80	14	*	6	-	present
Chicken Pass						
Glaucous-winged gull	*	*	*	*	*	22
300 Island (No Name)						
Glaucous-winged gull	70	-	*	242	522	588
Red-faced cormorant	-	74[1]	*	16	-	*
Nests	-	43[1]	*	7	-	*
Pelagic cormorant	-	63[1]	*	36	14	*
Nests	-	23[1]	*	14	*	*
Cormorant sp.	-	8[1]	*	-	17	*
Nests	-	12[1]	*	1	*	*
Horned puffin	60	-	*	13	12	*
Tufted puffin	500	-	*	51	80	present
Common murre	-	-	*	13	-	*
Pilot Rock						
Glaucous-winged gull	20	-	*	84	*	*
Horned puffin	30	-	*	11	*	*
Tufted puffin	10	-	*	14	*	*

Table 11. Species composition and abundance at seabird colonies in AMNWR for all surveys, 1976-2011. Colony survey locations are listed west to east, from Nuka Bay to Resurrection Bay. (continued)

Colony/Spp	1976	1986	2007	2009	2010	2011
Cheval Island						
Glaucous-winged gull	140	-	*	104	500	517
Red-faced cormorant	100	-	*	3	-	*
Nests	-	-	*	2	-	*
Double-crested cormorant	36	-	*	18	3	*
Nests	-	-	*	4	-	*
Pelagic cormorant	20	-	*	31	17	*
Nests	-	-	*	11	-	*
Cormorant sp.	-	7	*	1	-	*
Nests	-	-	*	20	-	*
Horned puffin	210	-	*	58	59	present
Tufted puffin	140	-	*	32	8	*
Common murre	-	-	*	4	1	*
Lone Rock						
Northern fulmar	40	30	*	*	-	*
Glaucous-winged gull	24	50	*	*	-	*
Horned puffin	40	2	*	*	-	*
Tufted puffin	80	20	*	*	-	*

[1] Average of counts from two visits

34

Table 12. Counts of black-legged kittiwakes at eight historic and two newly established plots in the Chiswell Islands (AMNWR), 2011. Individuals is the number of adult kittiwakes present within the plot boundaries. Nests are defined as nesting material with either a chick or adult sitting or standing on it. * Denotes a lack of data.

Kittiwake Plot		6/14	6/20	6/21	6/23	6/24	6/28	7/19	7/20	7/21	7/27	7/28	7/29
Beehive Plot A	Individuals	139	*	84	113	82	76	99	104	83	89	81	*
	Nests	58	*	59	57	57	53	53	42	44	47	39	*
Beehive Plot B	Individuals	41	*	37	42	41	42	42	40	41	42	37	*
	Nests	33	*	26	29	29	31	30	28	27	27	29	*
Beehive Plot C	Individuals	196	*	138	154	157	140	150	147	132	150	131	*
	Nests	85	*	104	104	113	98	90	93	89	91	86	*
Beehive Plot D	Individuals	113	*	98	89	92	89	98	98	88	93	107	*
	Nests	61	*	66	57	57	54	37	41	43	47	51	*
Chiswell Plot A	Individuals	112	*	97	105	61	81	93	103	98	*	105	90
	Nests	67	*	62	57	41	52	49	56	44	*	56	46
Chiswell Plot B	Individuals	150	*	99	84	113	138	102	100	139	*	130	99
	Nests	84	*	74	73	82	85	64	55	84	*	67	65
Beehive B Plot	Individuals	131	*	93	130	102	130	264	185	125	87	103	*
	Nests	70	*	48	66	66	74	57	71	61	59	57	*
Matushka Plot A	Individuals	51	43	51	35	43	39	28	31	25	24	20	*
	Nests	22	19	22	20	19	20	12	12	12	13	10	*
Matushka Plot B	Individuals	*	*	*	122	105	123	124	139	126	130	117	*
	Nests	*	*	*	88	74	88	74	81	77	75	70	*
Chiswell A Plot	Individuals	*	*	*	89	84	80	74	72	64	53	0	*
	Nests	*	*	*	47	48	56	79	28	26	22	1	*

Table 13. Counts of common murres at nine newly established murre plots in the Chiswell Islands, AK, 2011. * Denotes a lack of data.

Plot	6/16	6/20	6/21	6/23	6/24	6/28	7/19	7/20	7/21	7/27	7/28	7/29
COMU 001	116	*	0	99	12	64	109	117	105	126	118	*
COMU 002	59	*	46	36	0	50	8	38	43	40	56	*
COMU 003	15	*	0	11	2	0	0	0	12	10	7	*
COMU 004	37	*	22	35	33	54	41	46	59	*	37	38
COMU 005	*	41	39	2	43	52	6	8	32	24	16	*
COMU 006	*	132	165	32	141	212	134	151	161	168	128	*
COMU 007	*	*	101	102	130	140	73	71	169	*	73	66
COMU 008	*	*	*	103	0	180	140	150	141	*	145	164
COMU 009	*	*	*	200	0	108	170	178	125	*	167	158

Table 14. Counts of double-crested (DCCO), pelagic (PECO) and red-faced (RFCO) cormorants at seven cormorant plots in Resurrection Bay, Aialik Bay, and the Chiswell Islands in 2011. * Denotes a lack of data.

Plot	Species		June 13	16	17	20	21	23	24	27	28	July 18	19	20	21	22	23	26	27	28	29
COSP 001	DCCO	Ind	*	12	*	*	20	17	16	*	15	*	24	21	20	*	*	*	20	16	*
		Nests	*	12	*	*	16	17	16	*	14	*	18	17	17	*	*	*	17	16	*
COSP 001	PECO	Ind	*	33	*	*	37	42	36	*	26	*	39	54	57	*	*	*	49	25	*
		Nests	*	27	*	*	27	33	28	*	20	*	23	24	28	*	*	*	27	45	*
COSP 001	RFCO	Ind	*	0	*	*	0	0	0	*	0	*	0	0	0	*	*	*	0	1	*
		Nests	*	0	*	*	0	0	0	*	0	*	0	0	0	*	*	*	0	0	*
COSP 002	DCCO	Ind	*	26	*	*	34	47	63	*	57	*	34	46	60	*	*	*	*	26	55
		Nests	*	24	*	*	28	37	43	*	38	*	20	42	42	*	*	*	*	23	43
COSP 003	PECO	Ind	*	14	*	*	14	11	12	*	6	*	7	3	3	*	4	*	*	2	*
		Nests	*	12	*	*	11	10	10	*	6	*	4	3	2	*	2	*	*	2	*
COSP 004	DCCO	Ind	*	*	21	18	*	*	14	*	*	24	*	*	*	27	*	30	*	*	26
		Nests	*	*	18	13	*	*	14	*	*	16	*	*	*	22	*	28	*	*	26
COSP 005	RFCO	Ind	3	*	*	5	*	*	1	9	*	0	*	*	*	0	*	3	*	*	0
		Nests	1	*	*	3	*	*	1	0	*	0	*	*	*	0	*	0	*	*	0
COSP 005	PECO	Ind	6	*	*	11	*	*	14	8	*	11	*	*	*	10	*	11	*	*	10
		Nests	4	*	*	5	*	*	9	5	*	5	*	*	*	6	*	7	*	*	6
COSP 007	PECO	Ind	*	*	*	10	12	15	17	*	15	*	0	0	0	*	*	*	0	0	*
		Nests	*	*	*	10	11	12	12	*	9	*	0	0	0	*	*	*	0	0	*
COSP 008	PECO	Ind	*	*	*	28	19	20	17	*	13	*	10	9	7	*	*	*	3	7	*
		Nests	*	*	*	26	17	16	17	*	12	*	7	8	7	*	*	*	5	6	*

37

Table 15. Counts of double-crested (DCCO) and pelagic (PECO) cormorants at one cormorant plot at Cloudy Cape in 2011. * Denotes a lack of data.

Plot	Species		7/4	7/5	7/7	7/8	7/11	7/12	7/13	8/4	8/5
Cloudy B	DCCO	Individuals	30	30	37	38	22	19	18	11	12
		Nests	30	30	35	34	20	18	16	11	12
Cloudy B	PECO	Individuals	7	5	6	5	5	5	5	*	*
		Nests	7	5	6	5	4	4	5	*	*

Table 16. Counts of adult glaucous-winged gulls present within the boundaries of twelve plots in KEFJ and AMNWR in 2011. * Denotes a lack of data.

Plot	6/27	7/4	7/5	7/7	7/8	7/11	7/12	7/13	7/18	7/21	7/22	7/26	7/29	8/4	8/5
Steep Plot	*	*	*	104	111	70	62	95	*	*	*	*	*	133	109
Black Plot	*	*	*	145	121	138	120	102	*	*	*	*	*	210	104
Cloudy Plot A	*	126	112	170	237	148	202	149	*	*	*	*	*	185	176
Surok Plot A	*	*	*	83	99	59	80	60	*	*	*	*	*	82	74
Surok Plot B	*	*	*	70	97	45	80	56	*	*	*	*	*	94	78
Granite Plot A	*	*	*	121	158	129	58	177	*	*	*	*	*	213	169
Granite plot B	*	*	*	141	239	226	112	265	*	*	*	*	*	215	200
Chat Plot	79	*	*	*	*	*	*	*	144	220	188	176	206	261	193
No Name Plot A	*	*	*	*	*	*	*	*	89	*	107	128	95	129	103
No Name Plot B	*	*	*	*	*	*	*	*	115	*	223	168	166	193	166
Cheval Plot A	*	*	*	*	*	*	*	*	94	*	135	196	148	257	112
Cheval Plot B	*	*	*	*	*	*	*	*	99	*	129	166	163	181	137

www.ingramcontent.com/pod-product-compliance
Lightning Source LLC
Chambersburg PA
CBHW080920290526
45795CB00007BA/2599

* 9 781492 714811 *